DEACON
MINISTRY

Richard Dresselhaus

GPH®

Gospel Publishing House
Springfield, Missouri
02-0503

Scripture taken from the HOLY BIBLE, NEW INTERNATIONAL VERSION®. NIV®. Copyright ©1973, 1978, 1984 by International Bible Society. Used by permission of Zondervan. All rights reserved.

Chapter 7 was adapted from the seminar Conflict Management Training for Local Church Leadership ©2001 by Gary R. Allen. This material is also found in the *Leadership Development Unit—Gold Level* available from Gospel Publishing House.

Third Printing 2015

ISBN 978-0-88243-851-1

Printed in United States of America

CONTENTS

INTRODUCTION

I t is hoped that this manual will meet a real need in every church. Since positive action demands capable and prepared leadership, it is fitting that something be done to help train our laypeople to be come effective deacons.

The manual is written with the accent on practicality. The issues raised are those which typically confront the deacon board. It is hoped that deacons will find here the kind of help that will prepare them for the challenge of ministering to the church.

Each chapter is designed to serve as a study unit. Suggestions are given for group interaction and problem-solving opportunities. A pastor may wish to lead the deacon board through the manual over a seven-week period, using one chapter per week.

The first chapter presents the biblical basis for the ministry of the deacon. Outlined here, too, are some of the basic principles for effective spiritual leadership. These are given early since they undergird so much of what is said later in the text.

Chapter 2 deals with the New Testament qualifications for deacons. The list includes those given for elders and bishops (overseers) as well. A pastor may wish to stretch this chapter into several sessions.

In chapter 3, the deacon is viewed in the work as an administrator. Practical suggestions are offered (for example, agendas, procedures, reports, portfolios). In some instances, you will find help in setting up forms and reporting systems.

The role of the deacon as a servant is discussed in chapter 4. Since the deacon's main task is to serve, it is in order that some of the specific areas of service be dealt with. Visitation, ushering, counseling, and Communion service are some of the areas considered here.

Since the deacon is first a godly, Spirit-filled Christian, the fifth chapter is set aside to discuss the devotional and personal life of the deacon. What does a "devotional relationship" with God involve? How can the deacon's family be encouraged to participate in family time of worship and devotion? What place does the deacon's family have in this ministry?

The sixth and seventh chapters are designed to give the deacon opportunity to face life situations typical of those that anyone who is a deacon will confront in this ministry. It is hoped that these chapters will gather together the principles of effective spiritual leadership outlined in the earlier chapters and set them against the challenges that are faced in the deacon ministry.

CHAPTER 1

THE MINISTRY OF DEACONS

Y ou have been called to a high place of service in the church of Jesus Christ . . . the Lord has singled you out to be a deacon.

Congratulations!

And now the work begins—agendas, leaky roofs, parliamentary procedure, disgruntled members, balance sheets, and building programs—it is all a part of the job.

But you will enjoy it! Few offices in the church provide such a golden opportunity to do something significant for the kingdom of God.

Paul said to Timothy: "If anyone sets his heart on being an overseer, he desires a noble task" (1 Timothy 3:1). The same could be said for a deacon. Yours is a coveted position, and rightly so.

We begin with a survey of the role of the deacon as we find it delineated in the New Testament.

The Church Defined

The deacon's ministry is unto the Lord, but it is carried out within the context of the local church.

Two words must be defined:

Kuriakos: This is the Greek word from which we get the English word "church." It means "belonging to the Lord."

Ekklesia: This is the Greek word that is used repeatedly in the New Testament to signify the "assembly" of God's people. The word literally means "the called-out ones."

The Birth of the Church

When was the Church born? This is a question asked by scholars down through the centuries. Some say that the Church had its birth with the Ascension. Others argue convincingly for its birth on the Day Pentecost when the Holy Spirit was poured out.

Jesus spoke of the Church in Matthew 16:18 and 18:17, but in these passages He seems to suggest that its birth is yet future. Perhaps Jesus was speaking prophetically of that group of believers who would at a later time form His body, the Church.

When we come to the Book of Acts the picture becomes clear. Here the references point to a local gathering of believers who have come together for worship and instruction (Acts 5:11; 13:1; 18:22). Note, too, that Paul sent his epistles to specific groups of people in designated geographic areas.

The Church clearly has two sides: (1) the invisible side, which includes believers from every place and from every age, and (2) the visible church, which includes the local gathering of believers as they come together for worship and instruction.

The Nature of the Church

The church of Jesus Christ is an organism, "a holy temple in the Lord" and "a dwelling in which God lives by his Spirit" (Ephesians 2:21,22). It is the bride of Christ, the body of Christ, and the fellowship of the saints. It draws its life from its Head, the Lord Jesus Christ.

It is to the Church that the deacon is called. The deacon is to love the Church, be committed to its members, and be devoted to its mission. Every facet of its work is in the sphere of the deacon's concern.

Following are several implications of this truth for the deacon:

- The deacon always speaks well of the Church, knowing it is the body of Christ.
- The deacon's heart is set to serve the Church and see it prosper in every way.
- The deacon uses every resource to avoid rifts and division—and the ridicule and reproach that they bring.
- The deacon loves the Church, as Christ loves the Church, and is willing to give his life for her.

The Leadership of the Church

Jesus did not leave His church without leadership. Arising out of the New Testament narrative is a structure of organization that served the Church well in the first century. Under properly appointed leaders, the Church moved forward in unity and strength.

LEADERSHIP DEFINED

1. **Elders:** When churches were set in order during the first century, elders (*presbuteros*) were appointed to conduct the affairs of the local church (Acts 14:23). Literally, the word means "older men."
2. **Bishop:** The term bishop (*episkopos*) was used interchangeably with the term elder (Acts 20:17,28). Literally, the word means "overseer." It may be that the designation elder referred to the individual, while the term bishop referred to his office.

3. **Deacon:** The term deacon (*diakonos*) was used to designate one who was chosen to serve the members of the church. The deacon was by definition a servant. Paul called himself a servant, or "deacon," in 1 Corinthians 3:5 and Ephesians 3:7. Even Jesus was said to be a servant, or "deacon," according to Romans 15:8 and John 12:26. Paul told Timothy to be a good servant, or "deacon" (1 Timothy 4:6).

PATTERNS FOR TODAY

The Early Church had two offices to govern its affairs—the office of bishop/elder and the office of deacon. The elder/bishop was concerned with the general oversight of the work, while the deacon was called to serve in practical areas of ministry to the body.

In many churches, the eldership is help by the pastor or pastoral staff, and the lay leadership of the church is vested in the board of deacons. However, more recently, some churches have appointed a board of elders to serve the spiritual needs of the membership. The elders give themselves to prayer, ministry to the sick, counseling, and the discipline of members. The deacon board, in these cases, is then free to handle the more practical matters that concern the operation of the church. This does not mean, however, that the deacons ignore the spiritual needs of the church.

In this manual, it will be assumed that the pastor fulfills the role of elder/bishop, while those who comprise the official board fulfill the role of deacons. It should be noted further that in most churches the deacons act as the trustees of the church. In fact, some boards have an internal division—some are elected as deacons and some are elected as trustees. Throughout this manual, the "official board" will simply be termed "the board of deacons."

Duties of Deacons

The New Testament is not as explicit as we might like when it comes to a practical definition of the role of the deacon. What were the duties of the deacons who served in the Early Church? Who were the deacons? What were their specific duties? What was the manner of their selection and the tenure of their office? These questions press for answers that are not easy to find. A scriptural survey follows.

1. **Philippians 1:1**—Paul addressed this epistle to the bishops and deacons who were in the church at Philippi. The reference tells us only of the existence of their office well into the second half of the first century.

2. **First Timothy 3:8–10,12,13**—Here Paul set forth the qualifications for the office of deacon, but said nothing about their duties and responsibilities. We may properly assume that the office is generally recognized in the church by this time, but we are left in the dark as to its duties. First Timothy bears a slightly later date than the Book of Philippians.

3. **Romans 16:1**—This reference pushes us closer to the birth of the Church, but helps little to define the role of deacons in the Early Church. However, if by this rather early date the church had appointed a deaconess, it seems logical that the office of deacon was also known. This also shows that it is appropriate for women to serve as deacons.

4. **Acts 6:1–6**—Many see in this passage the New Testament pattern for what the church today calls the

office of deacon. Seven men were chosen to "wait on tables," thus freeing the apostles to carry on their ministry without hindrances.

It should be noted, however, that these appointed servants are not referred to as deacons. And, further, two of them, Philip and Stephen, became preachers of the gospel in only a short time.

EARLY FATHERS

The Early Church fathers shed some light on the role of deacons in the church of the first few centuries:

Ignatius: This man, a contemporary of John the apostle, states that the deacons were not mere servers of meat and drink. The inference here is that the role of the deacon was becoming a recognized office in the church by the end of the first century.

Irenaeus: The church in Irenaeus's day saw a clear pattern in Acts 6 and believed that the church should be under the direction of not more than seven men.

Council of New Caesarea: In AD 315, this council set seven as the accepted number for the group of men who administered the affairs of the church.

CONCLUSIONS

The New Testament is unclear about the actual duties and function of the deacons. However, judging from the composite of scriptural references and the testimony of the Early Church fathers, it is reasonably clear that the Early Church was served by a group of committed individuals who were called deacons, and that it was their duty to serve the church in whatever capacity those circumstances dictated.

Variations of the word *diakoneo*, "to serve," are found over a hundred times in the New Testament. Repetition points to emphasis. The Early Church saw the need for selected individuals to serve the body of Christ in practical matters.

In summary, the following inferences may be drawn:

1. The deacon was appointed to serve the church in any area of need that might arise.
2. The deacon was called to a supportive role in the spiritual ministry of the church.
3. The effectiveness of the deacon's service was determined by the measure of his commitments and faithfulness.
4. The deacon was expected to serve the church by the example of his character as well as by his deeds.

The Deacon Today

What can be said to help deacons become equipped for the task that faces them in today's church? Are there basic principles of Christian living that will help them be the kind of leaders God wants them to be? Isn't there a way to avoid those nasty pitfalls that so often claim the efforts of good people?

Yes, there are basic principles of Christian living that have special impact on those chosen of the Lord to lead His church. Some of them are listed here. They are basic principles to guide deacons in their calling as spiritual leaders.

I. SERVE IN THE POWER OF THE SPIRIT.

It has been suggested that a human being is tripartite— body, soul, and spirit. The body is that part that is seen and felt: the head, the legs, the arms. The soul is that part that is unseen but yet very real: it has to do with the personality, the emotions, the will, and the intellect—all those things that produce individuality. The spirit is also unseen, but most important, it is the place of communion with God.

The question here had to do with the level we function on in our service for God. Some people are motivated to serve God primarily for selfish reasons of gain. They hope to get rich, to make a sumptuous living doing God's work.

Others serve on the soulish level. They seek to make their mark by the power of their intellect, the force of their will, or the persuasiveness of their personality.

Unfortunately, too many of God's people live on this level. They are Christian humanists. They attempt to do God's work with might and power. The accent is on what they can do more than on what God can do.

The third level is the spirit level. Might and power are made to yield to a higher principle—the working of the Spirit.

Most of us have attempted to do God's work by vacillating between the second and third levels. We draw on all our human resources and set out to build the Kingdom. When that fails, we finally admit that only the Spirit can enable us to do the work of the Lord

The word *charismatic* is important at this point. When broken into its etymological parts it means "active grace" or "flowing grace." It simply means that the believer is but a channel through which God works by His Spirit. Pentecostal people are the people of the "flow through." The gifts and ministries of the Spirit flow out through their lives in blessing to the world.

Think of the tension that could be alleviated in the church if this principle were lived out. Think of the difference it would make as the deacon board grapples with the weighty issues of church leadership.

God has called you to be a deacon. Learn first that it is not by might or by power, but it is by the Spirit (Zechariah 4:6). It is a principle you cannot afford to violate in the work of God.

2. SPIRITUAL GROWTH COMES THROUGH CONFLICT.

A preacher once asked: "How does a Christian grow?" Then he paused.

While he paused I began to answer . . . inside myself: *By reading the Bible, through witnessing, by being faithful in worship—*

Then he answered with but one word: "Conflict."

I have thought about it often. And I have experienced the power of the truth repeatedly. It really is true. We grow through conflict.

On the surface it would seem to be good if we could enjoy perpetual tranquility. But would we grow? What makes a tree strong? What factors worked together to make Paul the man of faith that he became? If you took the conflict out of Peter's life, would you ever get the kind of man described in the Book of Acts? I think not.

We grow by conflict!

This may seem like an obvious principle, but it really works. It is when we find ourselves in a bind that we see how needy we are and how much we need God's grace.

It is when someone makes you wait that you see how impatient you are.

It is when someone falsely accuses you that you see how vindictive you are.

It is when someone won't let you have your way that you see how stubborn you are.

It is when someone ignores you that you see how insecure you are.

Conflict drives us to our knees and compels us to live near the Cross. Out of exposed need flows repentance and forgiveness. Conflict is the key.

Deacons have a golden opportunity to grow, for the will meets conflict along the way of service. If deacons resist conflict, seeing it as negative and insulting, they will crumble under their responsibilities. If they see conflict as a positive opportunity for growth, they will note with appreciation the spiritual growth in their own lives and the enhancing value of their contribution to the work of God.

It will help you to remember that the Cross is the place of conflict, but it was the occasion for the greatest of victories.

Obviously, do not seek conflict, but rejoice when it inevitably comes and learn to view it as a positive force that will move you on toward spiritual growth.

Growth comes through conflict!

3. KEEP YOUR SWORD IN THE SHEATH.

Peter had every reason to use his sword on the servant of the high priest. Was not his Lord and Master being threatened with death? He had every "right" to fight back—or did he?

Most of us fight for our rights. We draw a circle of defense around us and challenge anyone to step across the line. We contend for what we understand to be our personal rights. If our toes get stepped on, we seek revenge—our rights have been violated!

Jesus proved this principle by His example. He had every right in heaven and on earth to call down the angels and destroy the Roman soldiers that stripped Him of all self-respect and decency. But He didn't. He laid aside His human rights that He might fulfill the "right[ousness]" of the Father.

And we are called to do the same. As a spiritual leader you will be called upon to lay aside what could be clearly understood as your personal rights in order to meet a higher demand of service.

You will need to hold your temper when you have every "right" to speak.

You will be called upon to serve beyond the limits of logic and fairness.

You will be confronted repeatedly with the privilege of honoring others above yourself.

You will need to lay down your life, and its rights, to be a reflection of the One whom you serve.

Peter missed the mark. All he had to show for his payback attitude was a severed ear. And the last miracle that Jesus did before the Crucifixion was to put the ear back in its place.

And be sure of this: If you fight for your so-called rights, your trophies of victory will be no better than that of Peter.

Spiritual leaders are called to lay down their own rights so the righteousness of Jesus might be known.

4. LIVE IN THE LIGHT.

First John 1:7 says: "If we walk in the light, as he is in the light, we have fellowship with one another, and the blood of Jesus, his Son, purifies us from all sin."

The temptation is to live in isolation, to pull inside our shell and stay as hidden as possible. John said it ought not to be so with Christians. We are to walk in the light of divine revelation, and that involves horizontal as well as vertical relationships.

Too often suspicions and assumptions overcome the light of love and openness. Walls of misunderstanding and distrust are built. The people of God give themselves over to base feelings of vindictiveness and animosity, and the work of God falters.

The call of the Spirit is that the people of God live together in the light of Christ's love and grace. And spiritual leaders are to set the pace. As a deacon you are under obligation to live transparently and openly before those whom you lead. If you are to call others into the light, you must first dwell there yourself. A deacon board that adopts this principle as a practical guideline will find that their relationships together will be enhanced and their leadership among the people will be strengthened.

One of the most powerful prayers that a Christian can pray is this: "Let the Spirit of truth prevail." Since Jesus is Truth, it is in obeying Him that we find the answer to this prayer unfolding before us. We will, as John said, have true fellowship as we live together in light and love.

5. DARE TO ADMIT WRONG.

Board meetings have been deadlocked, churches split, and pastors sent on their way because no one was willing to admit having done wrong.

In principle, followers of Christ know that they are by nature wrong—wrong in their attitudes, wrong in their motives, wrong in their deeds. This is why they need God's continual grace. Though not sinning willfully, they are always conscious of their shortcomings and find that by admitting their basic wrongness they receive the abundant flow of God's grace.

Apply this to the ministry of the deacon who never forgets being vulnerable—never above error and always open to examination of the position of deacon. However, such openness does not in any way reflect indecisiveness but instead an awareness of one's own human nature. In other words, the ministry of deacon should be approached in a spirit of deep humility.

Always be prepared to say: "I could be wrong."

6. FORGIVE BEFORE YOU ARE ASKED TO FORGIVE.

When Jesus said from the cross, "Father, forgive them," there was no one in that crowd that was asking Him to forgive. Yet, He did! And so too must we. Some have called it "unilateral forgiveness," an extension of forgiveness that makes no demands on an erring believer.

A positive power is released when we do this. Just try it! In your heart forgive a brother or sister who is still at work to harm you. When you meet the offender again, you will find a tranquility of spirit that will communicate life and, hopefully, prompt repentance.

How sad and tragic when men and women in God's work hold grudges, waiting for others to produce "fruit in keeping with repentance" (Matthew 3:8). Neither gives in! The air gets tense. And months and years pass, waiting for someone to forgive first.

This principle brings freedom to spiritual leaders and puts them in a place where they can be greatly used to minister truth and love even to those who wrong them.

There are a host of equally valid and useful life principles that could be mentioned. But if spiritual leaders will consider even just these—and do them—God's work will feel the positive impact.

Again, congratulations! You have been called to serve in a high place. And the smaller you feel, the bigger that place will become.

You too can say: "I can do everything through him who gives me strength" (Philippians 4:13).

Suggestions for Group Study

DISCUSS:

- The operation of the church today must adapt itself to correct administrative procedures consistent with our times. The New Testament is a guide in spiritual matters but not necessarily in organizational matters. In other words, just because the Early Church had deacons does not mean that the church today should have deacons. Maybe there is a more streamlined way of doing things.

ILLUSTRATE:

- Try to find illustrations that will show how the life principles listed in the text work in everyday living. Has anyone ever tried to work with someone who could never be wrong? Has anyone experienced the effects of "unilateral forgiveness"?

APPLY:

- What can be gleaned from this chapter to make your work as a deacon more effective?

CHAPTER 2

THE QUALIFICATIONS FOR DEACONS

The New Testament presents a list of qualifications for elders, deacons, and bishops. Here we will put the lists together and come up with a composite of qualifications for spiritual leaders.

Gene Getz in *The Measure of a Man* lists these qualifications.[1] We will use his choice of terms for each qualification given by the apostle Paul.

Paul did not mince words when he laid down the requirements for spiritual leaders. As you go through these qualifications, you will likely feel very inadequate. In fact, you may wonder how you were chosen to be a spiritual leader. But don't forget, the Lord knows it is not so much what you are now but what you will become that matters most to Him.

Qualifications and Requirements

1. ABOVE REPROACH (1 TIMOTHY 3:2)

The emphasis here, as well as in Titus 1:6,7 and Acts 6:3, is on the person's reputation. How do personal acquaintances of the candidate for deacon regard the candidate? The believers in Lystra reported to Paul about Timothy, saying "the brothers at Lystra and Iconium spoke well of him" (Acts 16:2). A spiritual leader must have a good reputation. A positive impact on God's work will demand it.

A nominating committee, when evaluating nominees for the office of deacon, should inquire about each one's reputation. What do coworkers think about the nominee? Is the nominee regarded highly in the community? What is the reaction of family members?

2. HUSBAND OF ONE WIFE (1 TIMOTHY 3:2)

The Roman culture of Paul's day was accentuated with moral looseness much like we have in our day. In 1 Corinthians 5:1 Paul states that the immorality of the pagan culture had not only gotten into the church but had demonstrated itself in ways too shameful even for the pagans to comprehend. It is against this background that Paul writes.

Paul concluded that a man must be married to only one woman (and we might add, a woman should be married to only one man)—and the couple should be living together in tranquility, peace, and fulfillment. Some spiritual leaders have failed at this point. Unable to cope with the many temptations facing humanity today, they fall into sin. Satan delights in robbing people of spiritual authority by bringing them down in this area.

Getz provides five powerful guidelines:

a. We must develop good communication with our spouses.
b. We should not set up conflict situations by deliberately exposing ourselves to temptation.
c. We should fortify ourselves through regular study of the Word of God and prayer.
d. We must avoid unnecessary idleness.
e. We should seek help from someone we can trust if the problem seems beyond our control.

3. TEMPERATE (1 TIMOTHY 3:2)

The Greek word behind this qualification for spiritual leaders means "free from excess, passion, ruckus, confusion, etc., . . . well-balanced, self-controlled."[2] A spiritual leader is well-oriented mentally, socially, spiritually, and physically.

The power of God extends to every area of living. It is God's purpose, in Christ, to bring all peoples into harmony with Him, with themselves, and with their world. This makes for temperate individuals—usable by God in spiritual leadership.

4. SELF-CONTROLLED (I TIMOTHY 3:2; TITUS 1:8)

Since this word in the original has a degree of ambiguity as to its meaning, it is helpful to see Paul's use of the same word in Romans 12:3. Here Paul admonished the Roman believer: "Do not think of yourself more highly than you ought, but rather think of yourself with sober judgment." The Greek word translated "sober judgment" is the same word Paul used in 1 Timothy and Titus, but here it is translated *self-controlled*.

The point is clear. A spiritual leader is to be humble, willing to serve others, and accurate in self-evaluation. Such a leader realizes it is only the grace of God that constitutes and qualifies one's leadership.

5. RESPECTABLE (I TIMOTHY 3:2)

The Holy Spirit is very practical. Here He inspires Paul to speak of the importance of living a well-ordered life. The word *kosmios*, in its root form, means to "put in order . . . adorn, decorate."[3]

6. HOSPITABLE (I TIMOTHY 3:2; TITUS 1:8)

Behind these New Testament directives is Leviticus 19:33,34: "When an alien lives with you in your land, do not mistreat him. The alien living with you must be treated as one of your native-born. Love him as yourself."

What is your attitude toward your home? Have you given it to Christ for His use as He leads? A spiritual leader views hospitality not just as a social grace but as a way of bringing others into an atmosphere of Christian love and concern.

7. ABLE TO TEACH (I TIMOTHY 3:2; TITUS 1:9).

All of us know individuals who are well-informed, articulate, and gifted in the art of communication. Yet this qualification for spiritual leadership has more to do with the manner and quality of life than with special gifts of expression.

The word translated by this phrase "able to teach" (*didaktikos*) is also used by Paul in 2 Timothy 2:24. There the word is grouped with other designations that clearly refer to the quality and manner of life. Paul said that the servant of the Lord is not to be quarrelsome, but to be kind, forbearing, and gentle. All this is inferred in the word here translated "able to teach."

This point is powerful. A spiritual leader is to communicate Christ with all aspects of life. Attitude, industry, integrity, and behavior—all should speak of devotion to Him. In other words, one teaches by example, being an epistle of truth and life! People should be able to look at spiritual leaders and see Christ. What one does in this sense is more powerful than what one says.

8. NOT GIVEN TO DRUNKENNESS
(I TIMOTHY 3:2,3; TITUS 1:7)

The word used here (*paroinos*) means to *overdrink*, or to be *addicted* to wine. Although the reference here is not to total abstinence, the Bible elsewhere is very explicit in its warnings about the use of alcoholic beverages. (Note especially Proverbs 23:19–21, 29–34.)

Paul said: "It is better not to eat meat or drink wine or to do anything else that will cause your brother to fall" (Romans 14:21). In a culture like ours where drunkenness is prevalent, the spiritual leader will do well to avoid any conduct that could cause reproach to the work of God. Paul's admonition to the Ephesians puts the matter in positive perspective: "Do not get drunk on wine, which leads to debauchery. Instead, be filled with the Spirit" (Ephesians 5:18).

9. NOT OVERBEARING (TITUS 1:7)

Here Paul described the life of the self-centered individual. Others are merely considered servants. Their ideas never measure up. The spirit of such a person is one of control.

An effective spiritual leader is one who works well with others. If someone's idea counters his but is best for the group, it's accepted. Avoiding personal bias, others come first. Being effective means being a team player, one who looks at potentially divisive issues without knee-jerk reactions or foregone conclusions.

10. NOT QUICK-TEMPERED (TITUS 1:7)

Paul warned Titus to avoid those who have quick tempers, who are given to sudden outbursts of anger. Sinful anger has its roots in revenge and bitterness. It feeds on resentment. Many times God's work has been hindered by people who lacked self-control and were easily provoked to destructive expressions of anger.

Words are like feathers. They scatter easily and once scattered are impossible to collect. Outrage releases words of poison that corrupt and destroy whatever they touch. Every spiritual leader must practice self-control. He must rule his spirit and learn to hold his tongue from expressions of anger and vindictiveness. Temper tantrums and spiritual leadership are mutually exclusive.

11. NOT PUGNACIOUS (TITUS 1:7, NASB, OR "VIOLENT," NIV)

The King James Version has captured the meaning of the Greek word *plaktan* by translating it *striker*, one who physically lashes out at another. Here Paul spoke not of anger verbalized, but of anger out of control physically.

Cain was guilty of this sin and killed his brother, Abel. Moses was guilty of this sin and killed an Egyptian. Peter was guilty of this sin and attempted to kill the servant of the high priest.

God calls His servants to humility, self-control, and peace. Vented anger is not to be tolerated.

12. UNCONTENTIOUS (1 TIMOTHY 3:2,3, NASB)

The Greek word translated *uncontentious* is *amaichos*, meaning "peaceable" or "not quarrelsome."

Getz tells this story:

Tom is a smart, outgoing successful businessman. He is president of his own company . . . and is doing well—in fact, very well! . . . Six months ago Tom was elected to serve as an elder in his church, but there was something about Tom that no one really knew. As long as he was "calling the shots" and "making all the decisions," he was happy, easy to live with, and cooperative. But when he was just one among equals, it was a different story. . . . Tom always seemed to take an opposite point of view from everyone else on the board. If it was his idea, fine! But if the ideas came from someone else, he could never seem to get excited about it. . . . Needless to say, Tom literally destroyed the unity among this group of men. . . . He forced a vote on every issue, which usually came out 8 to 1 against Tom.[4]

The man of God is called to peace and not contention. Unfortunately, Tom had not learned this lesson. The work of God was impaired and so was Tom's own life.

13. GENTLE (I TIMOTHY 3:2,3)

Here is the antithesis of the three qualities noted above. Paul told us that the person of God is to be gentle. The original word, *epeikais*, means "yielding, gentle, kind, forbearing."[5]

All people are called to follow Jesus. He is the model. No one ever demonstrated such a gentle spirit as He. In the midst of mocking, slander, and ridicule, Jesus responded with gentleness and forbearance.

How does a person conduct himself when under pressure? When the membership makes unjust and undue demands, what then? In the heat of a tumultuous business session, how does one respond? The only proper answer to each of these questions is: in a spirit of gentleness and forbearance.

14. NOT A LOVER OF MONEY (I TIMOTHY 3:2,3)

The word behind this phrase is *aphilarguron*. It is composed of three parts: *a*—not; *phil*—love; and *arguron*—

silver, i.e., money. The admonition is pointed. Paul tells spiritual leaders: "Don't love money!"

Jesus taught: "Where your treasure is, there your heart will be also" (Matthew 6:21). Spiritual leaders must place their treasures under the control of Christ. All that they possess must be viewed as a God-given resource, given so it might be given back. The work of God is not to be thwarted by leadership that puts riches above the Kingdom and its growth.

15. ONE WHO MANAGES THE FAMILY WELL (1 TIMOTHY 3:2–4)

The measure of a head of a family is the family itself. One who has demonstrated leadership in the home will likely demonstrate leadership in the church.

The tragic stories of Eli, who refused to restrain his rebellious sons, and David, who contributed to the delinquency of Absalom through apparent neglect, should be a solemn warning to every person of God.

The home is the real test. One may succeed in business, politics, or education, but be unable to build a strong home. This person is not qualified to serve the Lord as a leader in the church.

16. A GOOD REPUTATION WITH OUTSIDERS (1 TIMOTHY 3:7)

The responsibilities of spiritual leaders reach beyond the walls of the church building. They live under the eye of a community at large. And their testimony for Christ must have a clear ring out there as well.

When selecting church leadership, this factor must be weighed. How do the neighbors feel about this individual? When that person is out of town on business, what is the report of his associates there? Can that person's lifestyle and manner stand the scrutiny of those outside the circle of close friends? It must!

"Be wise in the way you act . . . Let your conversation be always full of grace" (Colossians 4:5,6).

"Lead a quiet life . . . mind your own business . . . win the respect of outsiders" (1 Thessalonians 4:11,12).

"Live . . . good lives" (1 Peter 2:12).

17. ONE WHO LOVES WHAT IS GOOD (TITUS 1:7,8)

Some people have an eye for evil. They see the bad, that which is wrong, and those things that ought to be other than they are. But there are others who have an eye trained to spot the slightest good, a bit of positive influence, a ray of light and hope—and these are the ones that God chooses to lead His church.

The Scriptures say that evil is overcome by good (Romans 12:21). The mind is to think on things that are true, noble, right, pure, lovely, and admirable. (Philippians 4:8).

Love what is good. The call is for those trained and exercised in this vocation—those who can look at impossibilities and see the possible, at the hopeless and see hope, and at the fallen and see restoration.

18. UPRIGHT (TITUS 1:7,8)

This is a call for spiritual maturity, for those who have the psychological and spiritual balance to make "upright" decisions.

The word *upright* (*dikaios*) may refer to a person in a position of righteousness before God, or it may refer to practical righteousness, as when Joseph is described as "a righteous man" (Matthew 1:19).

In any event, the word suggests to spiritual leaders the imperative of a right vertical relationship with God and a right horizontal relationship with people.

Fairness and equity are necessities for effective spiritual leadership, and God's people have a right to demand its presence in their leaders.

19. HOLY (TITUS 1:7,8)

The original word here is *hosios*, meaning "devout, pious, pleasing to God."[6] The accent here is on God's choosing a person's life—being set aside for the work and pleasure of the Lord. As the furniture in the tabernacle was declared holy unto God, so the person of God is set apart for ministry to God and ministry to people

The practical holiness Paul spoke of is not a spirit of isolationism and separatism. The call is away from all that is immediate and of this earth so that the one the call comes to may go back into the world and win it to Christ. The most pious—truly pious—are the most involved in reaching the lost for Christ.

20. NOT BE A RECENT CONVERT (1 TIMOTHY 3:6)

Paul admonished Timothy to refrain from choosing new converts (*neophutos*) to fill places of spiritual leadership. His concern was not only for the church but for them. They may become conceited and filled with pride. Or they may become discouraged by the negative pressures that inevitably come.

The walk with God is a walk of growth and development, and it takes time. A new convert, while having great zeal, lacks the depth of understanding and wisdom that flow out of experience. When confronted with the pressures of leadership he will find it difficult to act decisively and wisely.

A caution is in order. This in no way refers to chronological age, nor, in fact, to time itself. Some people have "been in the way" for years, yet are "recent converts" in maturity. A person's qualifications for leadership should be weighed according to criteria measuring spiritual growth and development.

The Scriptures hold forth a high standard for spiritual leadership, but that is as it should be, for there is no work on earth so important to time and eternity as the building of Christ's kingdom through His body, the Church.

Suggestions for Group Study

DISCUSS:

1. Which of the requirements do you think are the most difficult to satisfy?
2. How does a deacon handle the problem of feeling unworthy and unqualified to fill this office?
3. Does God sometimes allow a person to be chosen as a deacon who has some obvious deficiencies in life?
4. Are there some qualifications in the list that you would single out as more important then others?
5. Are there qualifications you think should be added, or, if you were making out the list, what insertions and exclusions would there be?

PROJECT:

- Why not set up a program for "self-improvement" in the deacon board? Perhaps the deacons should meet regularly just to take an honest look at themselves in light of these qualifications. By helping each other, they could grow together and receive help in becoming the kind of leaders God has ordained them to be. Others can usually see our flaws more easily than we can.

ILLUSTRATION:

- As a group, put the apostle Paul against the list of requirements he gave and see how well he matches up to them. Can you find any areas of weakness? What are the obvious points of great strength? Do you feel comfortable knowing that Paul gave these requirements? That is, do you think Paul practiced what he preached?

Endnotes

[1] Gene A. Getz, *The Measure of a Man: A Practical Guide to Christian Maturity* (Glendale, CA: Gospel Light Regal Publications, 1974).

[2] William F. Arndt and F. Wilbur Gingrich, *Greek-English Lexicon of the New Testament*, 4th rev. ed. (Chicago: University of Chicago Press, 1957).

[3] Ibid.

[4] Getz, *The Measure of a Man*.

[5] Arndt and Gingrich, *Greek-English Lexicon*.

[6] Ibid.

CHAPTER 3

THE DEACON AS ADMINISTRATOR

Before discussing the deacon's role as an administrator, we will outline how deacons are selected in a church and what their terms of office are.

Selecting a Deacon

In most churches one of two methods is used in selecting the deacon board: by a nominating committee or nominations at the annual business meeting. And in many churches, both methods are used.

METHOD 1: A NOMINATING COMMITTEE

A nominating committee, recommended by the pastor and approved by the deacon board, presents in nomination the names of those who they feel meet the biblical qualifications to serve as deacons. The congregation, at its annual business meeting, selects from that list those who should serve. Of course, nominations from the floor are generally accepted.

This method has the strength of careful screening. The nominating committee may wish to interview prospective nominees, or they may work from a carefully prepared questionnaire. In either case, the names that go before the congregation have been prayerfully and thoughtfully chosen. This is a strong plus for this system of selecting deacons.

The following is a list of questions that should be answered by a nominee before his or her name is placed in nomination for the office of deacon:

- Do you know Christ as your personal Lord and Savior?
- Have you been baptized in the Holy Spirit, and

are you living a Spirit-controlled life to the best of your ability?

- Do you feel the Lord wants you to serve Him as a deacon?
- Do you understand that the deacon's ministry is that of service to the body of Christ?
- Are you prepared to submit yourself first to the Lord, then to His people, and finally to the other leaders you will work with?
- Do you support the local church with your tithes and offerings?
- Do you agree with the tenets of faith and governing principles of the church you belong to?
- Do you live a life that is consistent with the Word of God as pertains to morality?
- Do you conduct your home life in a way that meets with the demands of Scripture? Are your children in submission to God and the head of the home?
- If chosen, will you serve as a deacon in an attitude of love, unity, and faith?

If diligence is practiced in the selection process, those who are chosen will know that the office they are called to is one of great importance. Dare the church do less than put forth every effort to choose the right leadership to chart its course and set the pace? God's way is to have the right person in the right place at the right time. This is the key to the building of a great church!

METHOD 2: CONGREGATIONAL NOMINATION

A second method of selecting deacons is to have the congregation both nominate and elect them at its annual business meeting. This method is often used in a smaller congregation where nearly everyone is knowledgeable about those who qualify for the office of deacon.

The weakness of this method is obvious: it is impossible to screen nominees in a public meeting. Sometimes it is with embarrassment that a nominee must stand and refuse nomination. Or, more tragic than that, someone may be elected who is not qualified to hold the office of deacon.

On the positive side, this method gives the entire congregation the opportunity to be involved in the complete selection process. It prevents the existing board from attempts to propagate itself by carefully choosing the nominating committee.

Again, if the congregation is relatively small, this can perhaps be the most effective way of choosing deacons. Every church must evaluate its particular needs and then decide which method it should use.

In any event, great care must be taken in the all-important task of selecting leadership in the church.

The Term of Office

There are two approaches to the term of office for deacons in many churches.

1. SUCCESSIVE TERMS

Some churches elect deacons for a three-year term and upon the completion of that term the deacon may be re-elected for another three-year term.

The strengths are these:

- Retention of proven leadership
- Continuity and uniformity
- Stability and permanence

The weaknesses are these:
- Monopolization of leadership by a few individuals
- Lack of fresh, new ideas
- Difficulty in eliminating poor leadership

2. NONSUCCEEDING TERMS

Other churches elect deacons to a single three-year term. After the first three-year term, a person must step down for at least a year. Afterwards this person may be reelected for one more three-year term.

Generally speaking, for the reasons noted above, this is the most satisfactory way to handle the term of office for the deacon. Each church will need to decide which method will serve its needs best.

Assigning the Deacon's Portfolio

A wise pastor will immediately assign specific areas of responsibility to each deacon. The pastor should be careful to match talent with task, and may find it advantageous to talk to each deacon about personal strengths and weaknesses before assigning the deacon to an area.

This procedure will free the pastor to concentrate on the specific ministry he or she has been called to. It will give the deacon specific areas of service that have been defined for him or her.

Following is an example of the kind of breakdown that can work for a seven-member deacon board.

- Building and maintenance
- Ushering and Communion
- Sunday School
- Youth
- Missions
- Stewardship
- Music

Ministry areas can be added, changed, or combined to fit the needs of the individual local church. Each area should be delineated with enough detail so the deacon will fully understand what is necessary in discharging responsibilities. People serve best when they know precisely what is expected of them. A fuzzy job assignment will inevitably result in a slipshod performance.

Another thing to remember is the need for accountability. A pastor who asks for systematic reports will find that performance is greatly enhanced. There is also positive motivational value in demanding accountability. It makes one feel that the task is important and that someone cares. A wise pastor will devise a reporting system that will give the needed information and provide the deacon with a way to report the progress achieved in his area.

A sample monthly report form for missions is included here. These completed forms could be collected and discussed at each monthly board meeting.

DEACON'S MONTHLY REPORT
—MISSIONS—

Name
   John Jones

What was the gross income in missions for the month of May?
   $1,020.16

What is the percentage of increase or decrease over the same time period a year ago?
   13.5%

What future events involving missions should be placed on the church calendar?
   Convention, Oct. 10–15
   District Missions Rally, Sept. 16

What programs do you now envision for the future?
   An educational program
   Youth motivational seminar
   All-church missions banquet

Are there areas in your department that need full-board input?
   Underwriting budget for all-church missions banquets; appointment of a new missions secretary

What is your attitude toward your area of responsibility? Do you feel positive about it? Are you enjoying your work?
   I enjoy these responsibilities. The continual growth in missions is gratifying. I would like to see greater interest in US missions.

Obviously, each portfolio will need its own report form. And each pastor will want to use a form that will reflect the program that is compatible with the congregation. However, the above form will give a general guide to those pastors and deacons who choose to use a report form.

The congregation should be informed of the portfolio assignments. When they have questions in a given area, they can go to that deacon rather than seeking out the pastor for the needed information.

It may also be advisable for the deacons to have an opportunity at some time to make a summary report to the entire congregation. The annual business meeting provides a good occasion for this, if the reports are printed and kept brief.

Deacons' Meeting

The bylaws followed by many churches call for a monthly meeting of the deacon board. Larger churches may need to have additional meetings, as the need demands. And in any church, matters arise from time to time that will necessitate special meetings of the board of deacons.

Prior to the meeting, an agenda should be sent to each deacon. With the agenda items available prior to the meeting, the deacon is able to give thought and prayer to each matter before arriving at the meeting. A deacon board will make wiser decisions if they have adequate time to consider each issue ahead of time.

The following is a sample agenda for a typical board meeting:

MONTHLY MEETING OF THE OFFICIAL BOARD

OCTOBER 16, 7:00 P.M.
CONVENING IN PASTOR'S OFFICE

Devotions (A five-minute devotional thought by a deacon is good, followed by group prayer and worship.)

Minutes of last meeting

Financial report

Reports of deacons
    a. Building and maintenance
    b. Ushering and Communion
    c. Sunday School
    d. Youth
    e. Missions
    f. Stewardship
    g. Music
Action on reports

New business
    a. Acquisition of playground equipment
    b. Wage adjustments for secretarial staff
    c. Proposed purchase of kitchen equipment
    d. Candidates for membership
    e. Repair of roof over church office
Adjournment

Naturally, the agenda will be dictated by the matters that need action. It is not so important what form the agenda takes, as it is that there be an agenda. Too often board meetings freewheel and unnecessary time is taken. Deacons will learn to appreciate the efforts of the pastor as he attempts to facilitate board action by giving careful thought to the agenda.

DEACON'S NOTEBOOK

Wise decision making demands the immediate availability of relevant materials. For this reason, every deacon should maintain a notebook that will keep at his fingertips the resources needed for discussing and acting on matters that have to do with the operation and ministry of the church.

A loose-leaf notebook is preferable for this purpose. It may be well for the pastor to take the lead in this and provide for each deacon a notebook with the necessary labeled dividers. Suggested divisions are:

- Portfolio assignments
- Deacon reports
- Staff job descriptions
- Staff reports
- Agendas
- Board minutes
- Monthly financial reports
- Special reports

Each deacon is expected to keep his notebook current. When his term of office expires, he passes the notebook on to his successor. In this way, there is a continuity of information available for the new deacon.

A deacon will take pride in his work if he is trained to be efficient, and the availability of information is the key to making that efficiency possible.

FINANCIAL RECORDS

It has already been stated that careful record keeping is essential. However, a reminder of the importance of good financial records is in order.

The members of the congregation deserve to know how the finances of the church are being handled. A system must be devised that is workable, easily understood, and has "expandable potential" as the church grows. A professional system should be sought to be sure that the system being used is proper.

The Internal Revenue Service is becoming far more stringent in their requirements for nonprofit organizations. No church should give an occasion for questions to be raised. Sound principles of accounting are essential.

GENERAL OBSERVATIONS

It may be helpful to mention several matters that assist the deacons in their work together as a board:

1. Follow the accepted rules of parliamentary procedure. This will assure fairness in the decision-making process and will eliminate needless waste of time.
2. Be guided by a spirit of cooperation. The board of deacons should function as a team. "Unity amid diversity" must be a practical principle.
3. Maintain clear and complete records of actions taken at any regular or special meeting of the board of deacons.
4. Hold in strict confidence those decisions and discussions of the deacon board that call for confidentiality. Insensitivity in this area will

destroy the effectiveness of any church board. God's work rightfully demands the greatest care that one can give.

5. Grow together as brothers and sisters in Christ. Serving on the deacon board will provide the occasion for spiritual growth and development.

The Deacons and the Pastor

The New Testament makes it clear that the primary task of the deacon is to serve. And the pastor, as much as anyone, needs the deacons' help, looking to them for guidance and help in handling the affairs of the congregation.

The entire church will feel the positive effects of a strong and trusting relationship between the pastor and the board of deacons. The harmony that exists in this relationship will soon be copied by the membership of the church.

Following are several questions that should be asked.

1. WHO HAS FINAL AUTHORITY IN THE LOCAL CHURCH: THE PASTOR OR THE DEACON BOARD?

This is hardly a fair question. The Lord is the Head of the church. His is the final authority in the church. Yet He works through His people. It is His pleasure that the pastor, together and in harmony with the deacon board, seek the will of God for direction in handling the affairs of the church. A spirit of "submit[ting] to one another out of reverence for Christ" (Ephesians 5:21) should prevail. This is not, however, to lessen the place of the pastor as the under-shepherd over the household of God.

2. WHAT ARE THE RESPONSIBILITIES OF THE DEACON BOARD TO THE PASTOR IN MATTERS OF FINANCE?

The deacon board should be sensitive to the needs of the pastor in this area. An annual review of the pastor's salary and benefits is advisable. Increases in cost of living, positive performance of the pastor, and a comparable wage analysis should be taken into consideration in setting levels of compensation. A pastor should have faith that the Lord will supply his needs, and the deacon board should seek the Lord as to their response to his faith. Mutual respect and understanding are imperative on this sensitive issue.

3. IS IT NECESSARY FOR THE DEACON BOARD TO GIVE GIFTS TO THE PASTOR ON SPECIAL OCCASIONS?

This will be a matter for individual boards to determine. While a pastor should never expect any kind of special treatment, there may be occasions when courtesy and love would make the giving of a gift appropriate. There are many ways for a congregation to show their love and appreciation to the pastor, and an occasional gift may be a chosen way to do so. Never should such considerations as these become of major importance, either to the pastor or to the deacon board.

4. SHOULD THE DEACON BOARD MAINTAIN A RETIREMENT PROGRAM FOR THE PASTOR?

If possible, there should be positive action on this matter. Too often a pastor reaches retirement age and lacks the financial resources to provide for himself and his family's welfare. If a pastor has lived in a parsonage during the years of his ministry, he may be without a home at the time of his retirement. A systematic program of investment will eliminate this unfortunate circumstance. Many churches have developed flexible and practical plans for the retirement needs of the pastor.

5. SHOULD THE DEACON BOARD GRANT THE PASTOR LEAVE FOR STUDY AND PRAYER?

Most certainly it is. In addition to vacation time, a pastor should be allowed time away for study and prayer. One pastor is given two weeks per year for this purpose. He had commented that during this time he is able to read through a number of books and have time dedicated for prayer and meditation. Deacon boards should admonish their pastor to avail himself of this opportunity. The work of God will be blessed by it.

A Staff Manual

In some churches the pastor, in consultation with the deacon board, draws up a manual setting forth the guidelines for the pastor and the pastoral staff in order to eliminate misunderstandings and confusion. [Note: Many of these items may be covered in a church's constitution and bylaws.] The following is a suggested outline for such a manual:

1. Job descriptions—setting forth the scope of work
2. Working hours—giving the daily schedule for office hours
3. Hiring procedure—outlining the steps to be followed in filling a vacancy or employing an individual to fill a new position

4. Vacation time—stating the number of weeks per year that will be given for vacation
5. Sick time, leave of absence, and holidays—giving the guidelines in each of these areas
6. Termination—setting forth the responsibilities of the deacon board and the pastor or staff member in this regard

Each church will want to include additional items in its staff manual in harmony with its distinctive ministry as a church. However, every church, regardless of size, should have specific guidelines in these areas to eliminate misunderstandings and confusion.

A wise pastor will be sure that he and the deacon board have a clear understanding on these practical matters. To set forth guidelines will provide clarification before misunderstanding has occasion to arise.

Calling a Pastor

One of the most awesome responsibilities of the deacon board is to provide continued pastoral ministry in the church. When a pastor resigns, it becomes their responsibility to present to the congregation a nominee or nominees to fill the office of pastor.

GUIDELINES FOR FINDING A NEW PASTOR

1. Establish procedure. Who will chair the board in the absence of the pastor? Will a special committee be chosen to serve as a pulpit committee? Or will the deacon board act as the pulpit committee? Will the committee visit a prospective pastor's church prior to extending a call? How

many services will the prospective pastor conduct before an election is held?

2. Articulate the qualities of leadership that the church should have at this particular time.

3. Seek the will of the Lord in leading you to the person who possesses those qualities.

4. Vote on one candidate at a time. People become confused when they must choose between candidates. It is also unfair to a prospective pastor to be subjected to a competitive approach to the selection process.

5. Guide the people to make their choice prayerfully and thoughtfully, rather than on the basis of popularity or personal desire.

6. Share candidly with the prospective pastor what you, as a deacon board, feel to be the direction of the church and what you envision for the future.

The choice of a pastor is a most important task. The deacon board that earnestly seeks the Lord and follows a prayerfully developed procedure may be confident that God's person will be chosen to serve them as their spiritual leader.

QUESTIONS OF A NEW PASTOR

A new pastor will have many questions. These may be asked and answered in a candidate-deacon board meeting prior to the election, or they may be asked and answered after the candidate has been elected as pastor. The timing on this depends on the candidate and the deacon board.

Some questions a new pastor might have are:

1. Are there any limits on outside ministry?

2. What is the church's attitude toward the role of the pastor's spouse? What will his or her responsibilities be?

3. What is the procedure for compensation? How are church-related expenses handled? Is a parsonage provided or is a housing allowance given?

4. What is the church's policy on the pastor's participation in the denomination's sectional, district, and national activities?

5. How would the church feel about the pastor's involvement in a continuing educational program, working on an advanced degree, for example?

There are scores of other questions that need answers when a new pastor arrives, but these are at least indicative. The inclusion of this list of questions is to alert the deacon board to their responsibilities in working closely with a new pastor. It is a time of adjustment for the new pastor as well as for the congregation. Anything the board can do to facilitate that adjustment is time well spent.

Suggestions for Group Study

SELF-EXAMINATION:

1. Are the deacons' meetings you attend structured for the best utilization of time and to facilitate the decision-making process?

2. Do you have well-defined guidelines for the pastoral staff to follow?

3. Do you conduct an annual review of all salaries and benefits to be sure they are at the proper levels?

4. Do you as a deacon have an assigned area of responsibility?

5. Have you received guidance in fulfilling that responsibility?

6. Are there opportunities for the deacon board to meet together informally for fellowship and spiritual growth?

DISCUSS:

1. Should a deacon be able to serve consecutive terms as a member of the deacon board? If not, why not?
2. How long should a pastor remain in the same church? What are some of the values of a long pastorate?
3. Who do you feel has the final authority in the church? Do you think this is an unfair question? If so, why?
4. What are some positive suggestions for creating a worshipful attitude in a deacon board meeting? What place should be given to Bible study and prayer at the regular meetings?
5. In what ways can deacons help one another to grow spiritually?
6. What are some ways in which unity in the board can be achieved? Is it either possible or advisable to seek unanimity on every issue that is voted upon?

CHAPTER 4

THE DEACON AS SERVANT

The deacon must have a servant's heart.

Jesus did: "The Son of Man did not come to be served, but to serve, and to give his life as a ransom for many" (Matthew 20:28).

Paul did: "Though I am free and belong to no man, I make myself a slave to everyone, to win as many as possible" (1 Corinthians 9:19).

And you must too!

The Servant Principle

What is it that brings satisfaction in the Lord's work? Is it the size of the church you work in? Is it the honor and prestige of the office you hold? No, satisfaction in the Lord's work is wrapped up in one word—obedience!

The greatest delight of slaves is to please their master. That is the motivation of their lives. They spend themselves in service. Through servitude, workers enter the joy of their calling. Obedience becomes the only measure of success.

Servitude squelches competitiveness and cravings for self-exaltation and promotion. Servants live in dependence; their lives are dominated by their master. And it is in this that their joy is made complete.

Deacons must live out this principle. Their will is subordinated to the will of Christ. They place the well-being of others above their own. They have an eye for the needs of others. They are dominated by love and devotion to their Master.

A DEMONSTRATION OF SERVITUDE

John 13 tells the story. Jesus, facing the approaching cross, began to wash the feet of the disciples. All was well until He came to Peter: "You shall never wash my feet." Jesus said: "Unless I wash you, you have no part with me." To which Peter replied: "Then, Lord . . . not just my feet but my hands and my head as well!" (verses 8,9).

Then, at the end of the story, we read: "No servant is greater than his master, nor is a messenger greater than the one who sent him" (verse 16).

The message is clear: "You also should wash one another's feet" (verse 14). The call is to service!

Ministry through Ushering

First impressions are most important. How people are made to feel between the parking lot and the pew will directly affect their attitude toward the church and their ability to freely worship the Lord.

- If parking is a problem, was there anyone there to assist?
- Was there anyone at the door to offer a friendly smile and word of welcome?
- Was the church clean, tidy, and properly "climatized"?
- Was there someone there to assist them in locating a seat in the sanctuary?
- Did anyone offer assistance when they noticed the presence of a small child?

People must feel good about the way they are treated. It is the responsibility of leadership to be sure that coming to church is a pleasant experience for the worshipper.

What are the practical principles for effective ushering?

1. USHERING IS A MINISTRY TO THE LORD.

This is the first step. Those who accept a position on the ushering staff must feel in their hearts that their service is to the Lord. The acceptance of this principle will produce diligence and devotion. There is no greater service than service to the Lord. Ushers are called of God. Their work is the discharging of a divine commission.

2. TREAT THE WORSHIPPER AS A WELCOME GUEST.

Why is it that invited guests are given such careful consideration in homes but sometimes such careless treatment in church? A successful pastor challenged a group of ministers: "If a hundred new people came to your church next Sunday morning, would you be prepared to receive them?"

The point is well taken. Too often people are unattended as they shift for themselves in getting ready for the worship service—"Where is the nursery?" "Where are the restrooms?" "Can I find a seat in the back?" "What time does the service begin?"—and there is no one available to anticipate the questions and be ready with the answers. It is no wonder that some churches attract few new members from the community. They have not learned to treat new worshippers as welcome guests.

3. ORGANIZE.

Here is a checklist:

a. Has a head usher been appointed to coordinate the ushering program?
b. Does the head usher meet regularly with the pastor to coordinate the ushering program with him?

c. Are the ushers provided with a schedule to indicate when they are to serve?

d. Is there a training program in which the procedures of ushering are taught (e.g., seating people, receiving the offering, passing out bulletins)?

e. Is each usher prepared to give answers to the questions guests may ask?

4. LOOK THE PART.

Ushers should be dressed in neat, clean clothes. The culture of the church and surrounding community will help identify how dressed-up ushers should be. There should also be some way for guests to identify those who are there to help them (e.g., name badges).

The justification for a well-organized ushering program is clear. Worshippers must be freed from concerns so they may be free to worship the Lord. This is the objective of the usher's ministry.

Ministry through the Communion Service

The Communion service is an essential part of the church's spiritual life. It is that time when the body of Christ meets to celebrate the death, resurrection, and second coming of Jesus Christ. The deacon board will want to do its part to make that service what the Lord intended it to be.

Each pastor has his own preferred way of serving the emblems and conducting the Communion service. He will instruct the deacon board, and any others who may assist, in what is to be done to be sure the service flows smoothly and without needless interruption.

Just a few observations on the Communion service:

1. MAKE THE PROPER ARRANGEMENTS.

Be sure that someone prepares the emblems ahead of time and that the Communion table is attractively arranged. The trays should be polished, the table dusted, and the covering cloth, if used, clean and pressed.

2. AVOID ROUTINE.

Be flexible as the Holy Spirit directs. Prayer for the sick can be a part of the Communion service. It may be fitting for a member to speak of the significance of the Communion service to him personally. There are many possibilities for variation. Remember, too, that the Communion service may be held at any time when the church is together. Variety here may be good as well.

3. KNOW ITS SIGNIFICANCE.

In the Communion service, the body of Christ meets in celebration and fellowship. It is a time of rejoicing over the victory of the Cross and the blessed hope of the believer. It is also a time for the members of the body of Christ to renew their commitment to one another. Paul instructed the church: "For anyone who eats and drinks without recognizing the body of the Lord eats and drinks judgment on himself" (1 Corinthians 11:29). The Lord's body is not only the body of Jesus but now His body, the Church. The Communion service draws the members of the Church together in love and devotion, first to Christ and then to one another.

Ministry through Visitation

Deacons are called to serve. Part of that service will involve visitation. The dedicated deacon will not shrink from that responsibility.

There are some rules deacons should follow in visiting the members of the church they serve:

1. The visitation ministry of the deacon should be coordinated with the pastor. Since the total care of the congregation is the concern of the pastor, the deacons should inform the pastor of their efforts in visitation. The pastor's guidance will be of great value to the deacon.

2. The deacon should be careful that calls are well-timed and appropriate. People resent being bothered at mealtime, by unannounced visits, or with any contact that may be considered an interruption. A phone call will pave the way for a well-timed visit.

3. Lengthy visits are not usually advisable. Most people have demanding schedules and will appreciate the deacon's respect for their time.

4. Whenever possible, the deacon's spouse should accompany the deacon. Or the deacons may wish to accompany each other. Going "two by two" has many benefits and will eliminate potentially uncomfortable situations.

5. Deacons should be positive, supportive, and prayerful. They should refrain from involving themselves in conversations that will put others in a bad light or in any way create a negative impression of the church and its leadership

The deacon may be summoned to a home to pray for a member who is ill, to counsel with a member about difficulties in the home, to explain to a member the various opportunities for ministry in the church, or just to encourage a member by showing a personal interest in his spiritual growth and development.

The deacon will also be asked to call on members who have been hospitalized. The principles noted above are applicable for hospital calls as well. However, just a couple of further suggestions:

1. Plan to visit the patient during normal visiting hours. When possible, refrain from asking for special visitation privileges.
2. Keep the visit cheerful, positive, and brief. Remember, the patient may not feel well enough to enjoy a lengthy visit. A five-minute visit is usually adequate. Obviously, there are exceptions.
3. Avoid speaking to the patient about the details of his illness. That is the doctor's responsibility.
4. Close the visit with prayer. Believe that God is acting as you agree together for healing and encouragement.

Ministry through Counseling

The deacon is often called upon to fill the role of a counselor. His counsel may be sought at the altar as he prays with a member, during a house call, or at a chance meeting on any number of occasions. He will be asked to give advice in a variety of areas: domestic problems, church problems, spiritual problems, health problems, vocational problems, financial problems—just to mention a few.

Some deacons are well-qualified to meet the challenge of counseling. Others feel ill at ease and unsure of themselves as they attempt to fill this role. The following guidelines will be of value in helping the deacon understand some of the basics in this vital area of ministry to the church:

1. Learn to distinguish between the counseling a deacon should accept and that which belongs to the pastor. Do not hesitate to say, "I believe you should seek direction from the pastor on this problem." Most people will readily understand.

2. Remember that being a good listener is a fundamental principle in effective counseling. A deacon does not need to be highly skilled to listen with his mind and heart to the needs of a member in the church.

3. Hold the affairs of the membership in confidence. People with problems seek those counselors who will refrain from sharing personal information with others.

4. Maintain objectivity when counseling. Do not get emotionally involved or press the person to share information that may be inappropriate. Great sensitivity in this area is demanded.

5. Understand that the Holy Spirit will guide you when counseling. He is the Spirit of truth. He will enable those who earnestly seek God with a humble heart.

A deacon's ministry as a counselor can be most beneficial to the church if it is conducted with a deep sense of propriety. It is an area of vulnerability and ready pitfalls. The wise deacon will share with the pastor his progress and problems as a counselor. The pastor's encouragement and guidance will help the deacon make the most of this valuable opportunity.

Ministry to New Members

In many churches, the pastor presents a list of candidates for membership to the deacon board for their review and acceptance. The candidate is then presented to the church and given the right hand of fellowship. Sometimes this is all that happens—and it is up to the new member to discover what it means to be a member of the church.

The deacons can be of great assistance to the pastor in the process of bringing new people into the full membership of the church:

1. A training class for prospective members should be conducted by the pastor and attended by the deacons. The class may be held for several Sunday evenings just prior to the evening service. Or it may be scheduled for any other time that is mutually convenient. The class should deal with doctrine, membership requirements, church attendance, financial support, service opportunities, and church structure and practice.

2. The list of candidates should be divided among the members of the deacon board and each

candidate personally contacted to be sure that a wise decision can be made as to the candidate's acceptability for membership. This also has the advantage of giving the candidate a sense of belonging and a feeling that the church cares and take membership seriously.

3. In some churches, a special banquet is planned for deacons, pastors, and new members. This practice will place emphasis on the importance of church membership.

4. New members should be encouraged to find a place of ministry in the church. Some method should be devised to assess abilities and calling. A recommendation can be made as to an appropriate area of ministry. However, it is not always wise to push new members into responsibilities. They may need time to grow in the fellowship of the church before they accept some area of service in the church.

Good church members are not the product of chance. They are produced through the work of the Holy Spirit and careful and prayerful instruction and guidance. One of the many joys of being in spiritual leadership is to watch the members of the body of Christ grow into maturity and useful service for Christ. Deacons are key individuals in that process.

Ministry through Discipline

The pattern for church discipline is set forth in Matthew 18:15–17. The pattern contains the following provisions:

1. The offended party goes to the one who has given offense and speaks correctively about the sin. If the person who has been guilty of offense receives the correction, the matter is closed (verse 15).
2. When the offending party refuses correction, the offended one returns a second time, with a witness (verse 16).
3. If the offending party refuses "joint correction," the matter then goes to the entire church for their disposition (verse 17).

The Early Church understood the importance of church discipline. Ananias and Sapphira were found guilty of misrepresentation and thievery. Peter pronounced the judgment of God upon them (Acts 5:1–11). The New Testament is evidence that the Early Church practiced discipline in the care of its members. The apostle Paul instructed the leadership of the Corinthian church to expel from its membership a man who was conducting himself in an immoral way.

Unfortunately, the church today has often lost sight of the positive impact of properly executed discipline. Its members are sometimes left unchecked in their questionable conduct. The church, by virtue of its neglect, allows sin in its membership and stands by to watch itself being stripped of its authority and power. Great fear came upon the Early Church as a consequence of its disciplining action. Would not the same thing be true in the church today?

There are cautions and guidance that must be noted:

1. Pray for guidance. The biblical pattern is workable only in a spiritual context.

2. Act in unity and peace. If there is division among the deacons, nothing should be done until prayer has resolved the disunity.

3. Be redemptive in attitude. Paul's rather harsh treatment of the man in Corinth was intended to bring him to truth and repentance. Evidence in the Scriptures would suggest that he was eventually restored to fellowship. Discipline must never be vindictive and destructive. The goal is always redemptive.

4. Be quick to forgive. The Spirit of Jesus was one of forgiveness. He forgave before there was any indication of repentance. So too, we must we forgive from our hearts. Forgiveness, true forgiveness, means that we not only pardon the offender, but forget the offense. The deacon must have grace enough to do this.

Ministry by Example

The next chapter will deal with the deacon as a person. But it should be noted here that the strength of a deacon's ministry, in any of the areas discussed above, is largely dependent on the qualities of godliness that the deacon demonstrates. People learn best by looking at models. They do not hear with their ears nearly so effectively as they hear with their eyes. The deacon lives in a glass house and is being watched by the church and by the world.

It is just at this point that the deacon has an opportunity to be a powerful influence for the Lord. People are watching. That is good. Now they will see for themselves the power of God at work in a person's life.

Suggestions for Group Study

INTROSPECTION:

It is time to evaluate the areas of ministry discussed in this chapter as they are presently being conducted in your church.

1. What are the areas of strengths and weaknesses?
2. What are the underlying reasons for these apparent weaknesses and strengths?
3. What positive suggestions can be offered to strengthen the ministry of the church in each of these areas?

DISCUSS:

1. What prompts deacons to resist the servant role they are called to? Do they feel personally threatened by the thought of being a servant? Could it be an ego problem?
2. Why is it that some people are particular about the details of their personal lives but are indifferent about the details that affect the program of the church?
3. Why is it important that the pastor and each deacon maintain a positive and open relationship?
4. Do you agree that a deacon lives in a glass house? If so, in what sense? In light of this, what kind of life should the deacon live?

CHAPTER 5

THE DEACON AS PERSON

Deacons have been stereotyped. Somehow those who assume the role come out as not quite human. They have succumbed to a process of depersonalization and are hardly themselves.

This ought not to be. Deacons are first people—created like everyone else in the image of God. Then they are people of God—dedicated to Jesus Christ as Lord and Savior. And, last, they are servants of Christ to carry on His work on this earth.

They fit no mold, put on no airs, and create no images. They are simply people called of God to minister to the church. They dare to be human, they fit in, they enjoy living, and they are regular people. Away with all stereotyped notions of what deacons must appear to be that do not count. They are first and always God's choice doing what God wants. And that is enough—they can do nothing else.

This chapter is designed to explode any notion of stereotype, to show that deacons make a mark for God by being people, a whole people, God's people.

The Deacon's Commitment

There is a high cost for leadership.

Paul says that Jesus "made himself nothing" (Philippians 2:7). That, in summary, is the cost of leadership. Spiritual leaders must make themselves nothing, and that calls for commitment.

There are some questions that prospective deacons should ask themselves before allowing their names to be placed in nomination.

1. Can I place God's work above my own?
2. Can I put truth above personal popularity?
3. Can I accept accusations without demanding personal justification?
4. Can I absorb criticism without passing it on to others?
5. Can I hear gossip and not speak it to others?
6. Can I stand up for right although it puts me in the minority?

The deacon must consider the cost of accepting the call to leadership. The call demands a high level of personal and spiritual commitment.

The Deacon's Devotional Life

The Scriptures set forth a principle that will sustain the deacon in the most difficult and trying circumstances: "the one who is in [us] is greater than the one who is in the world" (1 John 4:4).

This means that the Lord has put within us a flow of power that is greater than the resistance of this world. What a promise for the spiritual leader! When the inner resource is strong, the challenge of ministry can never be too heavy.

I often tell myself, *Keep the inner flow strong!* That is the key. A spiritual leader who is strong in spirit can face with courage any obstacle that may come along. In this section of the manual that principle becomes the focus.

How can a deacon see this inner resource developed? How can one's spirit be strong in the power of Christ? How can one maintain a godly perspective and sense of priority amid the rush of living and serving? The answer is found in one's devotional life.

Here are suggestions that may be of help.

1. LIVE IN THE PRESENCE OF CHRIST.

There is no division between secular things and spiritual things in the life of a disciple. The deacon does not pass in and out of the presence of Christ, nor does he divide his church life from his daily life. He lives in the presence of Christ and views his entire life as a ministry unto God and people. His recreation, study, prayer, and meditations are viewed as one—it is all done as unto the Lord. It is part of that balanced view that spiritual leaders must understand and practice. One activity is never "more spiritual" than another if both are fulfilled in the will of God.

2. TAKE TIME TO BE ALONE.

Life on a treadmill does not build spiritual character. A child of God must have time to be quiet and alone. Being alone in meditation and prayer restores the spirit and sparks a new love for God and His work. It is the time to get it all together, to reflect, evaluate, ponder, dream, and expect—and it must be done alone.

This time should include supplication, intercession, and prayer. But it also should include time to listen, to be quiet before God, to look within, and to enjoy God. It might be called the "act of silence" or simply "learning to be still." In any case, it is a key to spiritual power and effective service.

3. LOVE THE WORD.

People who are grounded in the Scriptures are stable and strong. Their faith and service have found a footing. They are immovable and their lives have order and purpose. They have tapped a source of power that is renewable day by day.

As a practical suggestion for Bible reading, some have found it helpful to read passages from various parts of the Bible, in contrast to a through-the-Bible approach that runs from Genesis through to Revelation. A passage from the historical books, the poetical books, the prophets, the Gospels, and the epistles would give a balance to biblical studies that could be both interesting and helpful. Of course, this is a personal matter. The important thing is that the Bible be the "big Book" in the deacon's life.

4. EXPERIENCE THE DYNAMIC OF PRAYER.

Here is a mighty resource. Prayer knows no locked gates nor resistance to distance. It has no fear in the face of unbelief and dares to return time and time again. It is limitless in its power.

A visiting teacher shared the following outline for intercessory prayer. You may find it to be a guide to a new dimension of prayer:

a. Pray for those in leadership throughout the world.
b. Pray for spiritual leaders directly over you.
c. Pray for the city God has placed you in.
d. Pray for your nation.
e. Pray for the fellowship God has called you to.
f. Pray for your immediate family.
g. Pray for the lost whom God brings across your path.
h. Pray for new converts and needy Christians.
i. Pray for neighbors on your street.
j. Pray for those who speak against you or persecute you.

k. Pray for nations almost entirely unreached with the gospel.
l. Pray for those who are Communists, Buddhists, Hindus, Shintoists, and Muslims.
m. Pray for brothers and sisters in Christ who are without religious freedom.
n. Pray that your vision may be enlarged.
o. Pray for all the nations of the world.

Intercessory prayer has a worldwide impact. It knows no language or ethnic barriers. All it needs is a humble heart from which it may rise.

5. HAVE A REGULAR FAMILY ALTAR.

There is no substitute for it. A deacon who fails to pray with his family and read the Bible with them is guilty of the most serious kind of neglect. Time must be taken for this.

Here are some guidelines for family worship:

a. Involve every member of the family in some way. Even small children can contribute with a consenting smile or a clap of their hands.
b. Relate the worship time to daily living. What does the passage say to us in a practical way? How will its truths change our lives? What effect will our prayer time have on our lives?
c. Believe that Christ is at work. It is your place to stir faith in the hearts of your children. They must see that Christ is alive, that prayer does change things. Your attitude will prompt faith. You hold the key!

The Deacon's Spouse

Your spouse will share your call and ministry as a deacon if you provide the opportunity. Do you know that your spouse wants to share your burden, your heartaches, and your rejoicings? Your spouse wants to be involved—and will be if you provide that opportunity.

Not all spouses will be able to share in the deacon ministry. If you are a candidate for the deacon ministry, you should sit down and ensure that your spouse can support you in this important endeavor. Your spouse may not be able to be involved in every aspect, but at the very least offer encouragement and prayer support. Sharing of this ministry should be looked into well before you go forward with any candidacy.

Here are some tips for the deacon's spouse:

1. BE SUPPORTIVE.

There will be times when your friendly smile and word of encouragement will help your spouse over a difficult and trying time.

2. BE CONFIDENTIAL.

The matters discussed in a meeting of the deacon board are confidential. You will hurt the work of God by sharing information that is not yours to share.

3. BE HELPFUL.

Your spouse will need your counsel on many matters that pertain to the work of a deacon. Sharing matters with you, seeking your counsel, hearing your suggestions, and still knowing that those confidences will be kept are important aspects of support. You are a valuable resource for your spouse's ministry as a deacon.

4. BE FORGIVING.

You may feel resentful toward those who unjustly criticize the decisions of the deacon board, and a root of bitterness can begin to grow in your heart. This must not be allowed to happen. Learn to forgive and forget. Remember, bitterness will hurt you first—and then the work of God.

A deacon's spouse is a valuable asset to the work of God and should not be taken for granted or ignored. Spouses have much to offer. Their sensitivity and perceptiveness can be a great blessing to the person who carries on the work of a deacon.

The Deacon's Children

The measure of a parent is the children! You can tell a great deal about a father or mother by watching their children. They are a reflection of their parents' character and conduct.

Is it any wonder that the apostle Paul states emphatically that no man should attempt to rule the household of God until he first shows that he is able to rule his own house well? It is easily understood why Paul admonished spiritual leaders to keep their children in submission. Children are a credit or a liability to the ministry of any church leader.

But let's look at it from the children's side:

- "Don't do that—your father [or mother] is a deacon in the church!"
- "He sure doesn't act like a deacon's kid to me!"

- "Oh well, what can you expect from a deacon's kids!"

Is it any wonder that the children of deacons sometimes resent the role imposed on them? Is it too much to expect that the members of the church hold a consistent standard of conduct for all the children? It is tragic to single out any children and make demands upon them that are inconsistent with the standards for the entire group. Fairness is a must.

However, the children of a deacon should be very grateful that one of their parents is a deacon. They are often privileged to meet interesting spiritual leaders who come to their home. They are sometimes included in gatherings of Christian people because their parent is a deacon. And the blessing of having a godly father or mother, one who is qualified to serve as a deacon, is of no small consideration.

A wise deacon will take time to be with his children. He will play with them, do things with them, and develop a relationship of trust and love with them. There is no substitute for just being together and doing things together. The church is blessed by spiritual leaders who are part of a vibrant and spiritual family unit.

David was one of Israel's most dynamic leaders. He was a man after God's own heart. But he failed as a father.

It is possible that Absalom was raised by the servants in the palace, since David considered administering a nation more important than spending time with his son. There was possibly no time for a relationship of love and discipline to develop between David and Absalom.

At the news of Absalom's death, David cried out: "O my son Absalom! My son, my son Absalom! If only I had died instead of you" (2 Samuel 18:33).

It did not have to be. Though David was a spiritual giant, he failed in this very important area of life. He left to others a task that only he could do.

The warning is clear, and every deacon needs to reflect on this story. It shows the awful consequences of confused priorities and inverted values. Children must come before ministry in the church, for they are a sacred trust.

Here is the order of things:

- God, first
- Spouse, second
- Children, third
- Church, fourth

If you live by this order, God will be honored through your family and you will multiply your ministry through them.

The Deacon's Reputation

You have heard it said: "And he claims to be a deacon in the church!" Unfortunately, the reputation of the deacon in question does not complement his office or his testimony as a Christian.

All that you are either complements the work of the Lord or detracts from it. You live in a glass house, and people are watching you.

They want to see a faith that matters all week long and that is evidenced by a transformed life. They want to see Christ in you! When you said, "I accept the office I have been elected to," you placed on yourself this responsibility.

People rightfully expect something more from you. They will expect that your house complement the neighborhood and that you dress properly. They will expect that your word is as good as your signature. It is all a part of the office you hold.

The Deacon's Personality

The deacon's work is with people, and getting along well with them is of utmost importance.

One minister has said, "People must like you before you can minister to them." To an extent, that is true. At least, they must have a respect for you if they are to receive your ministry.

The prophets were despised, but they were honored and respected. This is the key. You are not in a popularity contest, but people must hold you in honor if they are to receive spiritual ministry from you. So, in a practical sense, your personality is vital to you effectiveness as a servant of the Lord.

Listed here are some principles for working with people that will help the person in the ministry of deacon:

1. MAINTAIN A SERVANT'S POSTURE.

Over and over this has been stated. But it is essential. The people you serve will follow your guidance if they sense that you have a high regard for their needs and are determined to help them in any way you can. Humility is a vital attribute in the deacon's life.

2. BE POSITIVE.

Any of us can walk into a committee meeting and greatly influence the atmosphere of the meeting just by our attitude. Don't say, "Looks like we shot ourselves in the foot again" or "I think we ought to get out of this while we still can" or "I'm really getting tired of seeing this item on the agenda."

Be assured the suggestion will cut like a knife of destruction. Instead, be positive: "The devil may be in the details for the world, but God has certainly been in the details of every project we've worked on!"

People gravitate toward positive people. They respond with joy and dedication if someone will just lead the way.

Remember, God is positive. He is bringing the world to a glorious consummation. He has the direction of history before Him and the last chapter is one of victory. Those who serve Him and work for the building of His kingdom must possess this attribute. Be positive, and view every problem as an opportunity.

3. KEEP THE GOAL IN MIND.

Someone has said: "So-and-so wins battles but loses wars." Have you seen this happening? I am sure you have—people who challenge every issue and drive it into the ground. With pride they say, "I won that round." But, unfortunately, people resist their leadership and they never fulfill their potential.

Always keep your eyes on the long-range program. Learn to give a little here and there to see the goal reached (assuming the compromise does not involve principle). You can prove you are right on a point, but if a person goes away insulted, you have lost a friend.

4. BE YOURSELF.

Don't "act like a deacon," however some people think one is to act. Just be God's person—yourself—free, relaxed, and confident in His grace. People will love you for it.

Don't forget, God has made you. Be pleased with His work and have confidence in yourself. Know that you can just be yourself and please God.

God's glory is best reflected in the lives of people who are confident of their standing in Christ; who know that all God wants is obedience and that the life of simple trust is enough to fulfill His plan.

5. RESPECT OTHERS.

People will often disagree with you. There will be people you find hard to appreciate. Yet, you must respect them and value their opinions and observations. They are also members of the body of Christ. Paul said that the parts of the Body that seem to be weak are indispensable, and that the Lord has tempered the Body together to form the composite that pleases Him. It is your privilege to serve the whole Body. Every member is important to God, and to you too.

6. DON'T RETALIATE.

There will be times when you will wish to fight back, but you cannot—for God has called you to be a leader. The Lord is your defense, and you need not feel that every accusation must be answered and every deed justified. It is the Lord's work. You represent Him. If your heart is right, He will vindicate you and the truth will march on.

You will be pleased at the response you will receive from most people if you are kind, loving, and willing to listen.

Usually all that people need is information and someone who is willing to listen. If you will maintain a spirit of respect and openness, the Holy Spirit will use you as a catalyst to maintain unity in the church you serve.

The Deacon's Reward

There is no higher joy than service. Jesus, because of the joy that was ahead of Him, endured the cross. His food was to do the will of the Father. On the cross, when Jesus said, "It is finished," all of heaven and earth were given cause to rejoice.

The deacon's reward is simply this: the realized joy of service. The deacon seeks no applause, trophies, or acclaim, but is satisfied just to know that he has been able to serve the people of God in love.

What is your motive in being a deacon? Are you bent on making a name for yourself? Is it your goal to put your stamp on the work of God so you will be applauded by others? Or do you fulfill your call for the sheer joy of knowing you are entering into Christ's will for your life?

The Scriptures warn us that we should not become "weary in doing good" (Galatians 6:9). Some Christians work and toil, give and strive, until in time they become exhausted and discouraged. This ought not to be. A pastor should sense this before it goes this far and put a stop to it. Deacons must not allow themselves to come to this place. They must keep the joy of service before themselves at all times. By living in the awareness that all efforts are for Christ and for the building of His kingdom, the deacon will not fall prey to this temptation.

Only eternity is going to show clearly the reward of the

faithful deacon and the measure of his ministry. The Lord has set the deacon in His church to carry on His work. Just to know that ought to be enough!

Suggestions for Group Study

PERSONAL PROJECTS:

1. Analyze your own personality. What do you see to be strengths and weaknesses? In your judgment, how do you get along with people? What can you do to make your relationships with others more constructive?

2. Consider each area of ministry outlined in this chapter and think through your personal adaptability to it. What can you do to be better prepared to serve in each area?

3. Evaluate the strengths and weaknesses in your relationship with your family. Is your family growing spiritually? Are you doing your part to lead the family in worship and prayer? Is the Bible an important book in your home?

DISCUSS:

1. Why is the deacon's family so important to his or her ministry?

2. Do you think that it is important that a deacon dress well, drive a clean car, and keep the lawn trimmed? If so, why?

3. Why do you think a deacon's devotional life is important?

CHAPTER 6

THE DEACON AS PROBLEM SOLVER

t's time now to apply the principles outlined in the previous chapters.

The problems raised in this chapter are typical of the complex and difficult matters that come to deacons for solution. The life situations cited here, while typical, are purely hypothetical. This chapter is intended only as a learning experience. It is important to remember that the pastor should be aware of any official action taken on matters such as the ones given here.

Problem 1

Suppose a deacon learns from reliable sources that a member of the congregation is involved in a financial scheme that is both dishonest and illegal. The member has been in the church for many years and has held places of responsibility in the past. He has a lovely family and is faithful to the church in attendance and support. What should the informed deacon do?

ALTERNATIVE ACTIONS:

- Take the matter to the deacon board for corrective action.
- Go to the member's wife and ask her to talk with her husband about his questionable conduct.
- Ask several of the key members their opinion about the matter.
- Just pray about it and do nothing.
- Take the matter lightly and share it with others as a point of conversation.
- Go to the pastor and let him decide what to do.
- Never tell anyone but use your influence to keep

the person out of places of responsibility in the church.

SUGGESTED APPROACH:

Matthew 18:15–17 provides the necessary guidelines. Go to the brother—no one else—and confront him with the matter. Deal with him in love and firmness. Be objective. Check your information to be sure it is correct. If he repents, the matter is closed. If not, follow the two additional steps outlined in Matthew 18.

After he has repented, you should counsel him to share this area of difficulty with his wife (if appropriate) and with the pastor. Both are entitled to this information, but it should come from him and not you.

Now, go back over the alternative actions and follow their effects. You will quickly discover that the biblical solution keeps the problem in perspective, does not hurt other people unnecessarily, is redemptive in its thrust, avoids gossip and false accusations, keeps the problem as small as possible, and does not hurt the church.

Problem 2

Suppose there is a growing awareness in the membership that the Sunday School superintendent should be replaced. The superintendent has served the church for years in an effective way. Likely he has simply grown weary with the responsibility and has ceased to be effective. Yet, he has not indicated his willingness to step aside. His two-year term will not expire for another eighteen months. What action should be taken?

ALTERNATIVE ACTIONS:

- Wait it out and at the end of his term vote someone else in to take his place.
- Discuss the matter freely among the members and hope that someone will leak the information that he is no longer wanted, and in that way force his resignation.
- Encourage, in subtle ways, a cool attitude toward the superintendent, hoping he will sense something is wrong and retire.
- Complain to the pastor until he is forced to replace him with someone more qualified.
- Commit the matter to the Lord and do nothing.
- Refuse to cooperate with any programs that originate with him.

SUGGESTED APPROACH:

The apostle Paul was forthright in his dealings with the church. He placed high value on truthfulness and openness and did not hesitate to give pointed admonitions to the leaders of the churches. He put the work of God above personalities.

The deacons and the pastor should weigh the matter, holding it before the Lord in prayer. Is it really true that this brother is as ineffective as it seems? Could he be challenged to approach his work with the zeal he once knew? Is there something bothering him that could easily be corrected if known? Or must he be replaced?

The deacons and the pastor, after prayer, should act. To do nothing is only to perpetuate the problem. If the superintendent must be replaced, it should be done with love and openness. On the other hand, if he can be helped to regain his previous effectiveness, that becomes a viable option. In any event, the board must be ready to act. If they do so in love, they can be confident that their decision will have a positive impact.

Now, go over the alternatives noted above and follow their possible effects. It is apparent that distrust, fear, pride, deception, and ignorance surround each in one way or another. Yet, such alternatives are sometimes followed, and with them come the sad effects of poor leadership decisions.

Problem 3

Suppose the pastor has brought upon himself the sharp criticism of many members of the church. His words are sometimes curt, he lacks sensitivity to the feelings of people, and he sometimes acts impulsively. In one way or another, he manages to alienate people from him. He is a good preacher and in many ways is an excellent pastor.

ALTERNATIVE ACTIONS:

- Encourage complaining members to be patient and wait it out.
- Cut the pastor's salary and hope he gets the hint and resigns.
- Be uncooperative and cool, and anticipate that he will either change or quit.
- Discuss the problem openly with other members to see if the negative feeling is widespread.
- Call a special meeting and force a resignation.
- Pray but take no action.

SUGGESTED APPROACH:

The Scriptures are clear: we are both to pray for those who have the spiritual leadership over us and to show high honor to those who are ministers for Christ. However, this in no way rules out the action of the deacon board of dealing with a very real problem. In this case, something must be done.

The deacon board should prayerfully discuss the problem with the pastor. He should be confronted with the reports that have come from the members. In some instances, it will be clear that supportive facts are missing, so these reports should be discounted. In a spirit of openness, the facts will emerge.

With correction must come the extension of forgiveness and restoration. The deacon board offers love and prayers. The situation can be cleared up and the work can go on. This is the ministry of the Holy Spirit to the body of Christ through its leadership.

Many ministries will be preserved if deacons will accept their responsibilities in ministering to the needs of their pastor. Their love and support will help the pastor to be the leader that God desires.

If you follow any of the alternatives noted above, you will readily see their folly. Yet, these alternatives are often pursued, with the result of churches being hurt, pastors discouraged, and the work of building the Kingdom seriously impaired.

Problem 4

Suppose the church is in the midst of a building program. Although both the pastor and the deacon board had felt satisfied that all construction costs were accurately projected, such was not the case. With the building 80 percent completed, the funds were depleted and construction ceased. The congregation began looking for explanations. The pastor and the deacon board felt defensive. A wedge was driven between leadership and the people. Something had to be done.

ALTERNATIVE ACTIONS:

- Continue the search for the people responsible for the incorrect cost estimates, and lay the blame at their feet.
- Call for new leadership. Ask for the resignation of the pastor and the deacon board.
- Discuss with others the irresponsibility of leadership and rally support for faultfinding.
- Pray but do nothing more.

SUGGESTED APPROACH:

Leadership must be accountable. The deacon board should assess its position. Why did the situation develop as it did? Who is responsible for the error? Was it clearly inadvertent and accidental?

A report should be made to the congregation by the deacon board. The report should be informative but not vindictive or faultfinding.

A positive solution should be offered to meet the problem. The entire congregation should be encouraged to rise to the occasion and believe God for an answer. A great problem can be turned into a great victory.

People respond to a challenge. With guidance, they will work together to see the project completed. The Holy Spirit has anointed leadership to rise to the occasion and bring forth a program that will lead to success.

Deacons who are nondefensive, filled with faith, ready to admit error, and prayerful will find a way to solve the most difficult problems. If you analyze the alternative solutions (i.e., actions) noted above, you will see they are well-worn but harmful to the work of God. They are in violation of the principles of leadership that have been outlined in this manual.

Problem 5

Suppose a neighboring assembly attracts to it some of the members of the congregation. A feeling of unrest fills the vacuum created by their departure. Rumors begin about why people are leaving and what is wrong with the church. The deacon board is in a quandary as to what should be done. There is fear that the exodus may continue.

ALTERNATIVE ACTIONS:

- Blame the pastor for failing to hold the people.
- Share in the discussion about "what's wrong with the church."
- Become embittered toward those who have left.
- Resent the pastor in the neighboring church.
- Try to discourage others from leaving by speaking ill of the people in the other church.

SUGGESTED APPROACH:

Any church will experience this situation from time to time. Granted, it is time for the deacon board and pastor to evaluate the ministry of the church, but it is not the occasion for panic. People do change churches for a variety of reasons. Their leaving does not necessarily indicate any failure in the church they have been attending.

Unless there have been areas of difficulty, people who leave should go with the blessings of the pastor and board. It is unwise to use any kind of force or coercion to get people to stay. If they feel it is time for them to leave, it is best to comply with their wishes.

Above all, be sure that no bitterness or jealousy is allowed to creep in. Speak well of other churches. Rejoice in their progress. Be supportive of what they are doing for Christ. It is all the Lord's work, and that is the compelling principle of all service.

Resentments sometimes follow a member who leaves to attend another assembly. This must not be. Everyone suffers when this is allowed to take place. A spirit of love and understanding must govern these matters.

Satan uses every negative occasion to further his cause, but the church must not fall prey. Rejoice over the work of God in every place, for it is the Lord's work and He will build His church.

Problem 6

Suppose a doctrinal controversy has developed in the church. Certain members have been influenced to follow the advocates of a "new truth." At this point, only a few members of the church are involved, but their influence is strong. The pastor and deacon board are united that something just be done.

ALTERNATIVE ACTIONS:

- Do nothing. Assume that the problem will disappear with the passing of time.
- Start a hostility crusade against the group that has apparently moved away from sound doctrine.
- Send each member who is involved a letter of disfellowship.
- Announce to the church that anyone involved in doctrinal controversy will be disciplined immediately.
- Call in the district officials to deal with the problem.

SUGGESTED APPROACH:

It is the charge of the pastor and deacon board to preserve the tenets of faith the church subscribes to. When members break from the tenets of faith the matter must be dealt with.

Some questions:

a. What is the exact nature of the so-called departure from the faith? Is the departure real or imagined?
b. Are those involved actually committed to this new doctrine, or are they only "inquirers"?
c. Is the doctrinal issue of consequence, or is it incidental to the general development of doctrine in the Bible?
d. Are the members involved militant and zealous in their approach to their new doctrinal insight? Are they influencing other members?
e. Is this doctrinal departure in direct conflict with the tenets of the faith the church subscribes to, or is it but a matter of interpretation?

Answers to these questions should be sought from the people whose conduct and beliefs are being questioned. A serious attempt should be made to understand exactly what they do believe and whether, in fact, there is a clear indication that wrong doctrine is involved.

Many times a doctrinal difficulty can be removed by a clear definition of terms. People may appear to have views quite different from ours, yet the differences evaporate when the issues are clearly articulated.

Be patient! Give people an opportunity to reevaluate. Perhaps they are momentarily impressed with some new teaching but will hold it only briefly. A wise pastor and deacon board will move cautiously and prayerfully in matters such as this.

However, if members can no longer subscribe to the basic tenets of faith that the church holds, it would be well for them to choose another fellowship. The pastor and deacon board should insist that their departure be in a context of love. It is wrong for animosity and bitterness to creep into situations like this. They need not!

Principles for Effective Problem Solving

What are the principles that lead to effective problem solving?

1. SEEK THE WILL OF GOD.

Deacons who make this a priority will find that they are effective as problem solvers. If the deacon uses a discerning spirit and an understanding heart, he will know the power of Christ and find that he is able to deal effectively with the areas of difficulty that arise.

- "Lord, what would you have me to do?"
- "Lord, let the Spirit of truth prevail."
- "Lord, open my heart to your ways."
- "Lord, give me your solution to this problem.

2. BE OBJECTIVE.

Wise deacons will not allow themselves to be caught in the emotions of the problems they work with. They must pursue truth and retain a sense of objectivity. As leaders, they do not have the option of speaking their minds and having the last word. Their mission is greater than winning an argument and establishing a specific point of view.

Deacons who allow themselves to become emotionally involved in the problems they face will be unable to see the alternatives clearly. They will act more from feeling than from fact. Objectivity is a must in the problem-solving process.

3. TAKE PEOPLE SERIOUSLY.

There is equality in the body of Christ. Every member is important. And it is the responsibility of leadership to take seriously the needs of each member.

Mutual respect goes a long way in solving problems and meeting the needs of members. If a member understands that there is a true concern for his area of difficulty, he will be helped and encouraged. Just to know that someone in leadership is taking his problem seriously is crucial to him.

4. BE UNDERSTANDING.

A listening ear is what many seek—just someone who will listen with both heart and ears. An effective leader identifies with people's needs and gives them the assurance that they are understood. Problems evaporate in an atmosphere of understanding and love.

5. KEEP THE PROBLEM SMALL.

- "My life is wrecked for good!"
- "The church will not survive this problem!"
- "I don't think I can make it."
- "This problem is too big for me to handle."

Wait! The problem has taken on inaccurate proportions. It has gotten way out of bounds. It isn't nearly so bad as it looks.

Wise leadership offers hope in the face of any problem. God does have an answer. He is at work in all things to produce good, for He is the Creator. You can whittle a huge problem down to size by showing that God has an answer. Faith always knows a way out. No problem is insurmountable.

This is a key to problem solving: keep the problem small. For it really is in light of God's greatness.

6. BE POSITIVE.

Negativism is one of the most destructive forces in the church today. People are quick to say, "It can't be done—it's no use keeping on!" Leadership must counter with faith and vision.

People get caught in a negativism syndrome. Negativism is like poison. It destroys whatever it touches.

Stay on the positive side of every problem. View problems as opportunities—for they really are—opportunities in which God will work!

You have been called of God to be a deacon. It is a high and wonderful call. Rejoice and be glad that the Lord has by His grace granted to you this privilege.

Yes, you will face many problems. There will be times of fear and doubt. But Christ has assured you that with His call come the necessary resources by which the call is fulfilled.

Have a thankful heart. It is good that the Lord has singled you out to be a deacon.

CHAPTER 7

THE DEACON AND CONFLICT MANAGEMENT

GARY R. ALLEN

This chapter will help deacons better understand the source and nature of conflict, and gain confidence in their leadership skills and ability to unify and effectively minister. As they depend on God's help, they can help other believers grow and develop; as the writer of Proverbs observed, "As iron sharpens iron, so one [person] sharpens another" (Proverbs 27:17)

The Source and Nature of Conflict

In the course of human interaction, conflict is inevitable as the result of fallen human nature. God's Word, however, is more concerned about how people interact and treat each other than in the fact that conflict exists.

As early as the account in Genesis 13 we find conflict among the herdsmen of Abram [Abraham] and the herdsmen of Lot. Abram averted the escalation of tension and destructive conflict when he told Lot, "Let's not have any quarreling between you and me, or between your herdsmen and mine, for we are brothers. Is not the whole land before you? Let's part company. If you go to the left, I'll go to the right; if you go to the right, I'll go to the left" (Genesis 13:8–10). Abram deferred to Lot for the good of their relationship and the good of the community of both families.

The Psalmist observed, "How good and pleasant it is when brothers live together in unity!" (Psalm 133:1). The term *when* implies there are times when unity does not exist among the brothers. Any human social group is likely to experience differences that can eventually become conflicting. The relational aspect of the local church is particularly vulnerable to conflict. Often, people become participants in a local church as the result of their personal relationship with Christ and enter into personal relationships with other believers. The Father's plan is for believers to disciple one another and reach out to unbelievers, bringing them into the community of faith. This close and personal interaction can produce periodic conflict.

Paul encouraged the Ephesians to maintain unity when he wrote, "As a prisoner for the Lord, then, I urge you to live a life worthy of the calling you have received. Be completely humble and gentle; be patient, bearing with one another in love. Make every effort to keep the unity of the Spirit through the bond of peace" (Ephesians 4:1–3). Paul realized that different people with different perceptions and values would eventually conflict even within the body of Christ. When conflict does emerge, however, the church should be able to manage conflict constructively, utilizing biblical understanding and interpersonal skills to find resolution.

Conflict is inevitable in human relationships when differences are not resolved in a timely manner. From these unresolved differences, conflict can emerge that will directly impact interpersonal relationships and social structure. If conflict is prolonged, it ceases being constructive or healthy conflict and becomes destructive.

HEALTHY CONFLICT

Healthy conflict can strengthen the unity and spirit of the people in the church, and, when this is done, the Spirit of God is given greater freedom to work through them. [1] The idea that conflict can bring positive results is usually difficult to believe for people in the midst of emotional discussions. When anger and aggression are channeled constructively, these energies help us mark our boundaries, define our identities, motivate our actions, clarify vulnerable feelings, and assert ourselves. [2]

When people think that all differences are destructive and that the ideal environment is when everyone thinks and acts the same, they create an atmosphere of unrealistic expectations. Then simple differences become exaggerated and become destructive conflict. It is important to distinguish between a *difficulty* (which we must accept and learn to live with, at least for the time being) and a *problem* in which we are stuck (created by mishandling a difficulty or smaller solvable problem). [3]

DESTRUCTIVE CONFLICT

The phrase "destructive conflict" can be defined as a protracted struggle or opposition between personalities, ideas, or interests. The key here is the word *protracted*. Differences, even clashes, between parties in a church do not in themselves constitute destructive conflict. These differences can be signs of vitality in a congregation. It is when they defy peaceful resolution and become protracted and entrenched in the life of the church that they become sinful and destructive. [4]

Conflict becomes negative and destructive when people become selfish and self-serving. Remember the observation by James about "desires that battle within" (James 4:1). When people want their way at the inconvenience and expense of others, they violate God's command to love and esteem one another. Such destructive conflict then becomes sinful and often needs the spiritual process of forgiveness to restore healthy relationships.

Destructive conflict in churches has increased dramatically in the past few years. Never before has division and discord been so threatening to the body of Christ. Destructive conflict in the local church:

- Undermines our witness. Belief that is not backed up with proper conduct is always unattractive.
- Drains precious time and resources. Fighting creates a massive hemorrhage in productivity and weakens our influence.
- Destroys relationships. Brothers and sisters in Christ are viewed as enemies to be vanquished instead of family to be cherished.
- Steals our motivation. Constant tension gives birth to pessimistic attitudes.

Destructive conflict appears to be a major hindrance in evangelizing unchurched people and assimilating them into the local church. H. B. London, Jr., vice president of Focus on the Family, suggests, "One of the reasons people use as an excuse not to attend a local church is the level of contention they observe. Pastors and Christian leaders must learn the art of managing conflict to [the point of] successful resolution if the church is to survive."[5] The unchurched do not expect the church to be free from conflict. However, it is not unreasonable for them to expect the church to resolve conflict with the same biblical principles the church proclaims.

Destructive conflict may be due to a number of factors. Whatever the causes of church conflict, it is important that Christians recognize the situation and determine, with God's help, to find resolution so that the church can provide effective ministry to the community.

Nine Common Causes for Church Conflict

1. People disagree about values and beliefs.
2. The [church] structure is unclear.
3. There is conflict over the pastor's role and responsibilities.
4. The structure no longer fits the congregation's size.
5. The pastor's leadership style is mismatched with the congregation.
6. A new pastor rushes into changes.
7. Communication lines are blocked.
8. Church people manage conflict poorly.
9. Disaffected members hold back [financial] participation and pledges. [6]

There are no quick fixes to conflict. Conflict management is an intentional process in which all participants commit to do what is right for the good of the whole church.

Reconciliation: A Foundation for Conflict Management

Reconciliation refers to the sinner being brought back into the presence of God. God made human beings in His own image so they could have fellowship with Him. But when human beings [they] sinned, they became strangers to God.[7] Christians, having experienced personal reconciliation with God, become ministers of reconciliation:

Therefore, if anyone is in Christ, he is a new creation; the old has gone, the new has come! All this is from God, who reconciled us to himself through Christ and gave us the ministry of reconciliation: that God was reconciling the world to himself in Christ, not counting men's sins against them. And he has committed to us the message of reconciliation. We are therefore Christ's ambassadors, as though God were making his appeal through us. We implore you on Christ's behalf: Be reconciled to God (2 Corinthians 5:17–20).

Christians as ministers of reconciliation are not only to proclaim the message of reconciliation to unbelievers but also are to live at peace with and be reconciled to one another in the community of faith. Jesus said, "If you are offering your gift at the altar and there remember that your brother has something against you, leave your gift there in front of the altar. First go and be reconciled to your brother; then come and offer your gift" (Matthew 5:23,24). Unchurched people seem to understand that conflict is inevitable even in the local church, but they do not understand why conflict cannot be readily resolved in the church when a major element of the gospel is reconciliation.

EVERYONE IS A MINISTER OF RECONCILIATION

Every Christian is a minister of reconciliation. The person who occupies the pulpit does not have one bit more responsibility in the ministry of reconciliation than a deacon or a child of God who sits in the pew, for Scripture says God has committed to us—pastor, deacon, Christian—the ministry of reconciliation.[8] The role of the pastor in this process is to see to it that everyone (including deacons) is equipped with the biblical knowledge of reconciliation and trained in relationship skills that facilitate reconciliation. They should be prepared to step in and work to restore those who are involved in a conflict.

The act of reconciliation is God's choice to enter into human confusion and hostility. It occurs because God is invited and eager to respond. But God, who knows each person's heart, responds in a way that creates reconciliation yet unheard of by either party. It may be necessary to set aside preconceived notions of reconciliation in order that God might be free to work in the destructive conflict situation.[9]

MINISTERS OF RECONCILIATION ARE PEACEMAKERS

Jesus described the ministers of reconciliation as "peacemakers." In the Beatitudes, He placed peacemaking high on the list of Christian characteristics when He said, "Blessed are the peacemakers, for they will be called sons of God" (Matthew 5:9). James described the harvest of those who sow in peace: "But the wisdom that comes from heaven is first of all pure; then peace-loving, considerate, submissive, full of mercy and good fruit, impartial and sincere. Peacemakers who sow in peace raise a harvest of righteousness" (James 3:17,18).

Not only is it expected that Christians will make peace with one another after relationships have been strained or broken, but they are also to be *peacekeepers*. Paul said that we are to make every human effort to get along with those around us and to live in peace: "Do not repay anyone evil for evil. Be careful to do what is right in the eyes of everybody. If it is possible, as far as it depends on you, live at peace with everyone" (Romans 12:17,18).

FORGIVENESS AS A PART OF CONFLICT MANAGEMENT

When conflict has been prolonged and people have hurt each other, forgiveness is necessary to reestablish healthy relationships. The term *forgiveness* is defined as "an active process of the mind and temper of a wronged person, by means of which he or she abolishes a moral hindrance to fellowship with the wrongdoer, and reestablishes the freedom and happiness of friendship."[10] There may be times when those in a conflicting situation refuse to forgive and reestablish fellowship, while others are willing to do so in order to facilitate their own healing process.

Jesus and Stephen are examples in forgiving their murderers even in the hour of death, when the attackers were unwilling to consider forgiveness and reconciliation. "Jesus said, 'Father, forgive them, for they do not know what they are doing'"(Luke 23:34). "While they were stoning him, Stephen prayed, 'Lord Jesus, receive my spirit.' Then he fell on his knees and cried out, 'Lord, do not hold this sin against them' " (Acts 7:59,60).

While most people probably will not face conflict unto death, destructive conflict can be one of life's most painful experiences. There are times when conflict may not be resolved, and forgiveness is necessary in order for the wounded person to bring closure to the situation and begin again. Some people willfully hurt others and have no intention of healing the relationship. Those who are wounded in such situations must learn to forgive those who have hurt them and move forward with their life.

However, forgiveness should not be used as a substitute for both parties engaging in the healing process if at all possible.

There is need for interpersonal reconciliation in the forgiveness process. The real work of forgiving is not just the release from hatred, resentment, suspicion, and hostility in the forgiver; it is found in regaining the sister and brother. Since the community of persons is the image of God, individuals are in relationship with others in order to express this communion. The principle "forgiveness is necessary, reconciliation is optional" is not based on the example of Jesus. Forgiveness that is focused on release from one's own conscience instead of on the restoration of community is not truly Christian. The goal is community restored, not private perfection maintained. [11]

Strategic timing is important in the forgiving process. Reconciliation is possible only when forgiveness is allowed time to work. Not allowing oneself the time needed to confront, face, and work through one's hurts might speed the goal of reconciliation but will not assure its quality. [12]

Two Biblical Models of Conflict Management

There are two primary biblical models of managing conflict. The first is a model for interpersonal conflict and the second is for conflict within the community of faith.

INTERPERSONAL CONFLICT MODEL

Conflict in the local church often results from unresolved personal differences. When brothers and sisters in the body of Christ realize something is wrong in a relationship, they should immediately address the matter. Jesus instructed His disciples in this matter (see Matthew 5:23,24). He indicated that our conflicts with one another must be resolved before we can approach God. Later in the Gospel of Matthew, Jesus described the appropriate procedure to follow when a fellow believer refuses to settle a dispute:

> If your brother sins against you, go and show him his fault, just between the two of you. If he listens to you, you have won your brother over. But if he will not listen, take one or two others along, so that "every matter may be established by the testimony of two or three witnesses." If he refuses to listen to them, tell it to the church; and if he refuses to listen even to the church, treat him as you would a pagan or a tax collector (Matthew 18:15–17).

Interpersonal conflict among those in the local church usually spills over into the whole church, affecting others and, too often, hindering the ministries of the church. When this happens, it is necessary to deal with the situation in a group setting.

GROUP CONFLICT MODEL

Conflict sometimes arises over ideas and beliefs that involve a group within the community or the whole constituency. Acts 15 presents a model for resolving conflicting issues that involved religious tradition and changing religious culture. The opinion of some that Gentiles should be circumcised had become divisive among the churches. The issue was presented before the apostles in Jerusalem, and a decision was made that became the guideline for the entire community of faith. Not all situations will be this clearly defined and readily resolved with such widely accepted support, but the biblical model is presented for the local church to emulate.

Differences and conflict are inevitable in the local church but are within the natural and normal boundaries of God's creation of free will and personal choice. Conflict becomes destructive to interpersonal relationships and organizational structure when people become selfish and self-serving in their interactions with others. Conflict is minimized and unity emerges when believers submit to one another in love and intentionally work toward what is right within the community of faith.

LEADERSHIP IS THE KEY TO CONFLICT MANAGEMENT

As Spirit-filled believers, we are familiar with transformation as we have been changed by the power of God from what we used to be into a new person in Jesus Christ. As Spirit-filled deacons, you can introduce others to this same transforming power and lead them into their personal transformational process of Christian discipleship and maturity.[13]

Styles of Conflict Management

There are at least five styles of conflict management, and every person has developed a primary conflict management style. However, each can learn to utilize all five basic styles to some extent, depending upon each given situation. The deacon needs to evaluate each conflict situation to determine which style would obtain the best results.

1. COLLABORATIVE STYLE

In contrast to the other styles, the collaborative style reflects a desire to fully satisfy the desires of both parties. It is based on the underlying philosophy of the win-win approach to conflict resolution, the belief that after conflict has been resolved, both sides should gain something of value. The deacon who uses a win-win approach is genuinely concerned about arriving at a settlement that meets the needs of both parties, or at least not badly damaging the welfare of the other side. When deacons use a collaborative approach to resolving conflict, the relationships between the parties are built on and improved.

The collaborative style is the approach an effective deacon is more likely to use because the outcome leads to increased productivity and satisfaction.

2. ACCOMMODATIVE STYLE

The accommodative style favors appeasement, or satisfying the other party's concerns without taking care of one's own. Those with this orientation may be generous or self-sacrificing just to maintain a relationship.

3. AVOIDANT STYLE

The avoider combines lack of cooperation and unassertiveness. The deacon is indifferent to the concerns of either party. The deacon may actually withdraw from conflict and just let things happen. An example of an avoider is a manager who stays out of a conflict between two team members, leaving them to resolve differences on their own.

4. COMPETITIVE STYLE

The competitive style is a desire to win at the expense of the other party, or to dominate. A person with a competitive orientation is likely to engage in a win-lose power struggle. This is not a good method for resolving church conflicts.

5. COMPROMISING OR SHARING STYLE

Sharers prefer moderate but incomplete satisfaction for both parties, which results in a compromise. The phrase "splitting the difference" reflects this orientation.[14]

The Cycle of Conflict

Dr. Norman Shawchuck, a church conflict consultant, describes a predictable five-stage cycle through which conflict usually passes.

STAGE 1: TENSION DEVELOPMENT

All conflict begins as a mere tension in the relationship. Tension signals that someone is sensing a loss of freedom within the relationship—and this perceived loss of freedom sets the stage for a conflict situation. Something is different in the relationship but it's hard to put a finger on it.

STAGE 2: ROLE DILEMMA

Confusion that develops as a result of tension provokes such questions as, "What am I doing to cause this tension? What is he or she doing? What's happening here? Who's in charge?"

STAGE 3: INJUSTICE COLLECTING

This is the first dangerous stage because people are convinced matters can only get worse. As a result they begin pulling apart and preparing for the battle that they are certain will come sooner or later. They begin collecting injustices and hurts that will be used as "artillery." Injustice collecting generates negative energy that must be dissipated before people will ever again be able to focus on the issue rather than on the "enemy."

This is the "blaming" stage where people begin justifying their own attitudes and behavior by pointing out the faults of others.

STAGE 4: CONFRONTATION

Confrontation may range from clearing the air to outright violence. In unmanaged conflict situations, people confront each other. In well-managed conflict, they confront the issues that caused the tension in the first place.

This is the fight, or *contact*, stage. The battle lines are set and conflict erupts. The contact stage is inevitable only after injustice collecting has gone on for some time.

STAGE 5: ADJUSTMENTS

Adjustments are the changes people make to end a confrontation. Seldom is there significant change without potential for increased conflict.

- Adjustments made in poorly managed confrontations are manifested as avoidance, divorce, domination, and cold war.
- Adjustments made in well-managed confrontations will take on the form of renegotiated

expectations and freely made commitments that honor the expectations.

If the adjustments made in this last stage are not adequate to resolve the conflict, the tension develops again and the cycle of conflict repeats itself. As this becomes a repetitive process, it creates a downward spiral of dysfunctional relationships that perpetuates destructive conflict and usually fragments the relationship to the point that resolution is nearly impossible.[15]

The Cycle of Conflict Management

The Cycle of Conflict Management was designed in response to the Conflict Cycle described by Norman Shawchuck above. The Cycle of Conflict Management is intended to be a process of reversing the downward spiral of tension development, role dilemma, injustice collecting, confrontation, and adjustments that can be so damaging to personal relationships and organizational structure. This process can also be beneficial as a preventative measure for conflict in the initial stage of tension development.

The process of the Cycle of Conflict Management includes five stages:

STAGE 1: TENSION DEFUSED

• Define tension. In an organization, healthy tension is in the diversity of people, ideas, and opinions that necessitate the clarifying of values, vision, mission, goals, and strategies. Unhealthy tension results when there is an effort to coerce or impose ideals and opinions upon others.

Tension can develop from the abuse of power. Control, authority, or influence is used to exert power. While control and authority may need to be exerted in special circumstances, influence is usually most effective for the strategic leader.[16] When tension develops there is a sense of injustice that often emerges from personal insecurities and wounded feelings. The injustice can surface from the past experiences and may not be directly connected to the present situation.

We can depend on the Holy Spirit to help us discern the dynamics and contributing factors in a conflicting situation and give keys to diffusing the situation: "Let us discern for ourselves what is right; let us learn together what is good" (Job 34:4). In Acts 5, the Holy Spirit revealed a selfish plot of deception. Peter's discernment, or knowledge, of what Ananias and Sapphira had done was a manifestation of the Spirit.

• Value diversity. To value diversity in the community of faith is to appreciate the culture of each other and establish unity that can defuse tension. Conflict can be avoided when basic differences are valued and accepted.

• Observe personality types, leadership and conflict management styles. Having a basic understanding of why people act the way they do is essential to maintaining unity within diversity. Utilizing various tools such as a personality type survey, a leadership styles survey, and a conflict-management-style survey can greatly reduce tension by helping people in the organization to better understand and appreciate each other.

Understanding the behavioral tendency of each basic personality type under stress will provide valuable insight as to why and how people act. Though it does not excuse inappropriate behavior, it allows a certain predictability of their response in a conflict situation. For example, the Dominant personality type will become autocratic, the Influencer will attack, the Steady will acquiesce, and the Compliant will avoid.[17]

• Disseminate vital and useful information to everyone. The church should maintain a consistent and thorough communication system. Vital and useful information empowers everyone. Tension develops when information is given only to a select few or is used to coerce others.

• Maintain an accessible feedback system. Leadership may better facilitate valid feedback by providing an open-door policy, allowing adequate discussion in meetings, and exhibiting an attitude of appreciation for opposing views. Often team members simply want to know that they are heard and respected.

The phrase "conflict prevention" may be used to describe the process of this stage. If the tension cannot be defused, however, it will progress to Role Dilemma (see above) and become a situation of conflict management.

STAGE 2: ROLE DEFINED

• Provide appropriate role descriptions. People work better when they understand their role and how they are expected to interact with others in the organization. Job descriptions enable participants to work effectively within the functional structure and accomplish the mission of the church more effectively. Vague job descriptions for staff and unstated role expectations for members leave all church parties vulnerable to conflicting assumptions about one another's callings.[18]

• Define expectations. Workers need to know exactly what is expected of them and to whom they are responsible. When people are uncertain about their roles and expectations, they may infringe on the roles and expectations of others and create unnecessary conflict.

• Give clear instructions. Knowing the boundaries of their authority and having clear instructions that give decisive direction enable workers to concentrate on the effectiveness of their efforts. Knowing the boundaries of their fellow workers will minimize conflict.

• Commit to mutual accountability. Those in leadership who expect accountability from the community of faith but are not accountable to those whom they serve will quickly lose respect and credibility within the community. Loss of respect and credibility will certainly lead to interpersonal and organizational conflict.

STAGE 3: JUSTICE DISPERSED

• Distinguish between equality and fairness. Often, the first impulse of leadership is to treat people equally. But each person is distinct. By treating people equally, their personal development and ministry within the organization may be limited. Therefore, it is important to know each other well enough to provide the kind of leadership necessary to help people to be most effective in their ministry.

• Demonstrate fairness. Leaders must be fair to everyone. To verbalize fairness and then intentionally discriminate among people will destroy the authenticity and credibility of leadership. When the leader is fair, those whom he or she serves are more likely to be fair with each other.

• Be expeditious in decisions. Trust and unity are developed, maintained, and reinforced when decisions are made as quickly as feasible. Delay in making necessary decisions will frustrate team effort, threaten trust in leadership, and fragment unity.

There may be times when the decision is to do nothing—waiting for a greater degree of openness in the group in order to find a better opportunity of intervention.

• Be quick to admit errors and make appropriate adjustments. The personal pride of the leader can get in the way of admitting wrong, expressing regret, asking for forgiveness, and changing behavior. When leaders are quick to demonstrate humility and ask for forgiveness, they influence others to do the same.

STAGE 4: COLLABORATION

• Involve everyone who needs to know. Everyone who is involved in the conflict needs to be a part of the solution. Those who "need to know" are composed of everyone who has been directly affected by the conflict and its process of resolution.

• Facilitate participation and ownership of all involved. Every participant must have a sense of ownership of the information, the conflict management process, and the resolution. When only a few within the group are viewed as owners of the situation, others in the group will be disenfranchised, setting the stage for tension and more conflict.

• Insure that all relevant information is obtained and available. It is the responsibility of leadership to gather the facts and maintain focus on the information that is germane to the situation. Irrelevant information will slow the process and create diversions. Everyone in the process must have access to the same information to avoid possible manipulation of power and control.

• Facilitate open discussion. Everyone must be free to state their perspective and ask relevant questions without the fear of reprisal. The group must be free from coercion and intimidation.

STAGE 5: ADJUSTMENTS

• Clearly define the adjustments. Determine what needs to be done and why. It is usually helpful to define, state, and rephrase the adjustments until they are clear to everyone. Putting them in writing may prove most beneficial for immediate clarity and future reference.

Adjustments should be in response to the primary conflict at hand. Adjustments that include only side issues to the main conflict can be interpreted as avoidant, superficial, and will probably reignite tension.

• Utilize a consensual process. Formulate decisions by involving everyone who is a stakeholder in the situation. Any process that disenfranchises any of the participants will create tension and risk beginning another cycle of conflict.

• Disseminate vital and useful information to the entire organization. When vital and useful information is disseminated throughout the organization, the potential for future conflict is minimized. Most conflict resolution results in some degree of personal and organizational change. However, change is not really change until everyone in the organization understands and embraces it.

• Affirm the people. People need to know they are valuable and appreciated. They will be willing to continue to participate in an organizational process that works if they know they are as important as the issues and the processes.

• Affirm the process. When people realize that the process has worked well, they will continue to utilize it and will be more likely to influence others in a positive manner toward the process in future conflict situations.

The Cycle of Conflict Management can be a helpful tool as an ongoing process of conflict management for the local church. If it is continually utilized, it can avert many conflicting situations and minimize conflicts that do arise.

Conclusion

Conflict management is the responsibility of everyone in the church. It is essential that everyone make every possible effort to minimize destructive conflict and be committed to one another in love. "If it is possible, as far as it depends on you, live at peace with everyone" (Romans 12:18).

When a congregation is no longer in destructive conflict, it will be indicated in the relationships of the people by:

- An energizing effect from participating in and talking about their congregation.
- Open communication with few restrictions on what can be talked about.
- Confidence that the leaders, fellow members, and the organization as a whole listen and respond to needs.
- A sense of growing as a group toward maturity and greater faithfulness.
- An effective adaptation to a changing world.[19] In understanding the source and nature of conflict and the process of conflict management, we can

better confront conflict with less fear and with the hope for resolution that strengthens personal relationships and enables the ministry of the church to be more effective.

Endnotes

[1] Norman Shawchuck, *How to Manage Conflict in the Church: Understanding and Managing Conflict* (Leith, ND: Spiritual Growth Resources, 1983), 12.

[2] Kenneth A. Halstead, *From Stuck to Unstuck: Overcoming Congregational Impasse* (Washington, D.C.: Alban Institute Publication, 1998), 42.

[3] Ibid., 77.

[4] Marshall Shelley, ed. *Leading Your Church Through Conflict and Reconciliation* (Minneapolis: Bethany House, 1997), 39.

[5] H. B. London, Jr., "Trinity College and Theological Seminary 2006–2007 Catalog," http://www.trinitysem.edu/Catalog_111606_rev120506.pdf. (accessed May 2009).

[6] Roy Pneuman, *Nine Common Sources of Church Conflict* (*Action Information*, March April 1992, 1–3), quoted in *Pastor we need to talk!* by Dennis Hester, http://www.betterchurches.com/chap02.pdf (accessed February 2009).

[7] Manford G. Gutzke, *Plain Talk about Christian Words* (Grand Rapids: Zondervan, 1965), 71.

[8] Dwight J. Pentecost, *Things Which Become Sound Doctrine* (Grand Rapids: Zondervan, 1970), 91.

[9] Joan Mueller, *Is Forgiveness Possible?* (Collegeville, MN: The Liturgical Press, 1998), 80.

[10] Lewis B. Smedes, *Forgive and Forget: Healing the Hurts We Don't Deserve* (New York: Pocket Books, 1984), 50.

[11] David Augsburger, *Caring Enough to Forgive: True and False Forgiveness* (Ventura, CA: Regal Books, 1981), 32–40.

[12] Doris Donnelly, *Learning To Forgive* (Nashville: Abingdon Press, 1979), 84–89.

[13] Phillip V. Lewis, *Transformational Leadership: a New Model for Total Church Involvement* (Nashville: Broadman and Holman, 1996), vi.

[14] *Team Building: Leader's Guide* (Atlanta, GA: Walk Through The Bible Ministries, 1993), 21.

[15] Shawchuck, *How to Manage Conflict,* 12.

[16] John H. Spurling, "Strategic Leadership" (Lecture at Assemblies of God Theological Seminary, Springfield, MO: June 2000).

[17] *Team Building,* 21.

[18] Hugh F. Halverstadt, *Managing Church Conflict* (Louisville, KY: Westminster/John Knox Press, 1991), 3.

[19] Halstead, *From Stuck to Unstuck,* 13,14.